WITH ALL THE SPACE REMOVED

nila christi

Copyright © 2017 Nila Christi
All rights reserved.
ISBN:0692979336
ISBN-13:9780692979334

So, I guess this is where I'm supposed to redundantly state
The Copyrighted Status of this book
and low-key threaten you to respect The Status
and bow down to me.
Okay. Cool.
I have a few issues.
Each one of them sings so much to me.
I'd make love to each and every one of them individually on a bed of thistles
just to feel, once more, the space they've claimed within me. (Not really.)
But I can't. So I wrote this book.
And now, They Who Steal My Crazy
will be forever cursed
with Dandelions of Abundance
(and children) blooming endlessly across their lawn.
They will be cursed
with The Unvision and will forever view
these fairy wishes as weeds
whom offer no medicinal stone
or backdrop for jazz music they'd never listen to otherwise.
(My favorite jazz musician is Thelonious Monk.
He has the best name and is filled with so much wisdom.
I will write fondly of him in the present tense forever.)
And I guess, like, if you steal my crazy…
I'll send My Lawyer
—that I have in real life—
to go after you
and steal my crazy right back from you
and give it back to me.
But you know what?
If you want my crazy that badly…
you can have it, Man.
I've got enough to go around.
Slap my crazy all over town.
Post it on the internet—
don't give me any credit for it.
Promise me you'll make a crown
with all those wildflowers.
They multiply like hell.
You'll have enough to go around. <3

To those

who see

in the eyes

of

The Other

& C...
"I finished this one
for you."
;)

Ingredients

Embody
Waiting Room
Nerve Ending
(Not) My Wedding Dress
This Ain't Seattle and This Ain't Outer Space
My Olivine
Let Me Tell You All About the Blanket on My Bed
Only an Aeronaut Might Know
Re-plugged, the Acoustic Version
Phosphorous
Abasement for Rent
Those Nights You Gave to Me
How He Likes to be Kissed
Let's Not Talk About the Main Course
One Day I'll Fly Again
How to Engrave Your Life
Whore Story
Apology as Allergy
Art is Outlawed
Friendly Reminder
We Got in Trouble
Rest in Pieces Assured, These Were Not Good Times
I Have a Small Room with a Dead Fly in it
Filling Out
New Vacancy
No More Lonely in the Stables
Coffee, Cake, and Cigarettes
Green Turquoise
Seriously Serrated
Life After the First Place
The One About the Body and the Bee
You Used to Teach Enlightenment
Not No, Yes
I Am Not a Marionette
Only Me
Extra Spectral Display of Confetti
For
Free Will to Follow
Miss Unwonderful

(More) Ingredients

On Losing Friends
Ditched for Glitter in the Gutter
Speaking of a Masquerade…
No, She Hasn't
Sender Bender
Desserts in Europe
I See Stars in the Sink
Is This Where I Quote Nietzsche?
Sit and Wait
Seeds of Soul
Your Hand
As Once, So Forever
Rafinesque Manatee (AKA The Stripper Anthem)
Hey, Loser, Clean the Kitchen
I Think We All Have Bad Tattoos
The Moon Slit Her Wrists by Sunset's Request for More Color in the Sky
I Need Therapy After Going to Therapy
Four-Fifty is Greater Than Seven
And Then I Got That Call About the Weather
To Freeze
S'More Love
I Used to Say Things Like "Casual Get Together." Wow.
Dug
We Flew to the Other Side of the World to Stand Outside the Planetarium
A Book Called Ghost Town
Some Thoughts from When I was Driving Home from Home the Other Day
(It's a Long Story)
Around Again
Four Fifty-Six AM with Thirteen Seconds Left
I Say to the Girl…
Not Much Like a Butterfly
The Cheapest Extermination
When Sickness Steals These Nights
Firm Habits
Rx Dreams
Let's Call it "Nightlife"
Cokehead. Cigarette Butt.
I'd Rather be Blind
Fast Fever Flying High
My Moldy Smile
Is She Shining?
Crack Like a Geode

(Even More) Ingredients

Heave-ho the Clothes of the Hefty Ho
The Zero's Prophecy
From My Mouth
Stillborn. Still Here.
Icky Situation
To Where Rain Hails
Metamorphosis: The New Girl
In My Room
Other Things That Make the Fall a Tumble Worth Tripping
Just What I Wanted
Tear the Wait
My Likeness Looks a Lot Like You
Return of the Roach

Embody

Dear Someone Else,

      I want to wake up in your body,
be canvas to the thread count,
      brush another number onto you.

      Coil the snakes that hiss you unrest,
weave dreams with your hands,
      collect them in your hollowed mattress
          of a heart I know a side door to.

Leave Me.

Love,
Me

Waiting Room

I watch them pirouette
                                          across the wall.

    Unimpressed.
        Glass crystals
                drip liquid
      poison
    from the web of dust
              dressed in neglect
      they tried
to spray away…

                Don't go
                    thinkin'
                        I didn't roll out
                                the welcome rug
        for you.

It doesn't matter how clean you are.
        You can never get close enough
                for them to leave you alone.
Those buggers have known home
        longer than the earth itself,
      back when you were just a shell
            of seed
    who rose a Kingdom of Thorn
            to deflower them of being.

Sage!, Lavender!
                    Let's cleanse this atmosphere!
                    This air here needs to hold us
    both,
                      both you and me.

        Breathe.
            Don't hold your breath.

                    Don't make a tunnel
                of your vision, wishin'
                  you could stop
                        it hittin' you
                            so hard
                            it numbs the hurt.

Soon enough,
            your time will cry,
                kick red regret
                      clay up from the dirt,
        run so fast it flies
    like Words spun
from the Lair of Mouth
        and out of mind,
    forgettin' all
        you've ever heard.
Your Soul
        will leave you
    hangin' there,
        rock 'n' roll
    right through
your ribcage,
    flown from a place
        you've never been.
All the soft wounds
        will heal you
                and the deep ones
                    will disappear
                        into the air
            of Never Again.
        Before then,
            there's this—
                The Danced Years
                    you can't dismiss.
    Mistake a misstep
        for a stair,
            twist when it's your turn
                to twirl, block the exits!

           The past would not exist
        without the future
              point of reference
                             first
                                     to know the difference.

           Shh!

           If it gets too loud just
                                  SHOUT!

     I'll always be right
                        here,
        and you'll be

"Next!"

Nerve Ending

Rectangular room's so artificially warm
    it could fuck your sperm count.
Hosts some hot guy with Black Onyx hair, immaculate eyes…
        and I'm locked in.
            Sitting right across from him.

    He's too young to be dressed in all blue.
    He's like, twenty-five, at the very oldest. Or twenty-six.

    I hold his handshake for a fraction too long.
        I let go
    only when he does,
    and I make believe it was my idea.

He asks me sexual questions in a decidedly nonsexual way.
Well, nothing too kinky, but overtly personal nonetheless.
    Like, how many partners have I had,
and-if-the-answer-is-more-than-zero,-am-I-*always!*-safe?,-and-am-I-*always!*-careful?,-and-when-was-my-last-menstrual-period-anyway?,-and-is-there-any-chance-I-may-be-pregnant-*right-now*?

    !   ?   !

    And I'd be lying if I said it didn't stir in me
        something that's been dormant for so long…

    I return all his questions with the Truth
    when I so easily could've served him lies.

    Damn it.   I should've lied.

But oh well. It's too late now.
    That's a phrase I feel I've just about maxed out on.

                Shoulda got up earlier.
                Brushed my hair.
                And my teeth.

Flossed.
Put on fresh jeans.
But oh well. It's too late now.
Shoulda flown to school today.
Started my homework the night before
I finished the last drop had dripped me dry.
It's gone.
But oh well. It's too late now.
Shoulda paced myself.
I want more.
Maybe started at the end,
swam back around to the beginning
without ever hittin' the middle,
thinkin' how long I've been at this
riddle-in words
shoulda solved it,
learned my lesson before it's too late...
But oh well. It's too late now.

   Am I acing this test?

I try to find takeaway in those eyes
scanning sheets on a clipboard.
   Forget those notes!
Those rods and cones have read what's written
                            on my insides.
Those retinas retain all my answers
               but relinquish none of his own.

They keep their charm but become a little less
exciting when those initial questions are replaced by less titillating
ones, and he's forced to address the cigarette
burn marks on my forearm and wonder if I've ever tried
to cremate myself to death.

   Should I lie?

Ten minutes later,

>I sit on the edge of my new bed,
>>sipping some pink smoothie thing.
>It's an awful appetizer, and it reeks
>>of vitamins and minerals.
>>>But whatever. I steel myself to the taste.

"I think Someone's got a crush on David,"
>>The First Woman says to The Second One,
>>>nodding her head in my direction.

>>The Second One smiles.
"*Mmm.* Isn't he *dreamy?*"

>I didn't know I had enough blood left in me,
>but I shy burn the same color as the chalky cocktail.

Ten seconds later,

>the empty cup rings a hollow echo
>on the windowpane.

"Wow, you drank that fast,"
>The First Woman says.

>>>>*What's the point of going slowly,*
>>>>*if I can't get sleep until I hurry up?*

"I don't want you to get a stomach ache,"
The Second Woman says.

>>>>*What do you care?*
>>>>*It's not your nerve ending to feel.*
>>>>*And me? I'm used to this kind of stuff.*
>>>>*Yeah, it sucks.*
>>>>*But like, oh well...*
>>>>*Ya know?*
>>>>*I'll deal.*

(Not) My Wedding Dress

They tell me how it's gonna be.
Fold a white nightgown on my sheet.
It's sheer.
It's too thin for me.

Nonsense.
It's been sewn for everybody.

This fabric of life's a robe
I'll wear religiously,
every morning's noon-lit sky to night.
And in between
there shall be nothing left
to separate me from what they see
as they record the numbers of my heart's strength,
rhythm, and what my framework's worth to them.

Okay.
Fine.
I've survived worse.

And worse yet has become
of those who answer to another Me.

It hurt,
I'm sure,
when words were stapled
to the wood of Truth—
a tree
whose crown would crest
to bless the rest of us.

He'd bleed.
We'd bow.
Cold sweat.

Maybe I'm ahead of myself.
Maybe none of this has even happened   yet.

This Ain't Seattle and This Ain't Outer Space

A voice sounds in my ear.

"Can I meet her?"

"Not now, dear.
There'll be time enough for that later."

They take a blade to the back of my hand.
    My limb railing's run dry;
  it's the only place I'll still bleed.
      Not with ease.
    Each try's a collision in traffic,
    metal vessel to osteo median.
Casualty,
    another failed attempt
        to drive.
Casually,
    they proceed,
    like it's no big deal.
      I'm still alive,
    like surely, they've done this before.
        My skin's a funeral of sores,
          bruises already blue.

"I see you."

"No, we're beyond that. Move,"

The Head says
    to a busy member of The Body.

"Hold this."

A torn fabric rolled tight,
    tied into a knot.
I'm supposed to wrap my fist around the cloth,
    until each manual phalanx can't beg
for liquid relief of life signs any louder.

If I haven't screamed out yet
    I never will.

They find a way to coast into my veins.

    Take what they need from me.

        And leave.

My Olivine

                          Twiggy branch of limb
                  escapes under the partition,
            tears the cloth that separates us
        like bedsheets from mourning to the side.
      My windows rise like I would on the outside
    to graze the lake of sea green invitations of her…
Lucky, I am still alive.

"I'm Olivine."

    She's a pretty thing.
        Battered child, blunt around the edges.
    Soft core apple bruises in all the inside places.
      Hard sharpness of high cheekbones
          and hipbones and collarbones
                    the kid could cut you with.
                She dances
            every time she drinks.
                She coughs
            every time she laughs
          with too much feeling,
    and I think every time she feels too much
              her spirit smokes
      another one in loving memory,
hiccups!, remembering how things used to be
in harmony. She sang,
    before she moved away,
        the melody.
        Before her home was here
                with me,
      in our room—it isn't much.
              She sang my name,
        said,
      "Nice to meet you."

Let Me Tell You All About the Blanket on My Bed

It is not one of security.
    No.
I left that one at home
next to my pillow that holds
    the picture of my headspace
        and a few strayed strands.
    Because I lose my hair now, don't I?

This blanket.
    It is not mine.
    It was given to me.
    It is the same as everyone else's.
    It is not unique.
    It is the same.

This blanket.
    Wears thin.
        Not *too* warm.
        Its stitches warp to weft a web to weave me up.
                In hostage?
                No.

This blanket.
    White, pattern-less
        is stained
        with the tattoo of my blood.
    Not the blood of being a woman, no.
        Because we are a girl now, aren't we?

This red   bleeds one that's taken from me,
    given
    daily, every day.
    Gorging needle in my vein.
        Sink me in.
        Suck me dry.

      Sip up all my platelets,
spit something else in their place.
     Unzip my river channels
with a sharp, un-violent
    slip
     into cold flesh, too warm-starved
       to really give what you're asking.

This blanket.
   It wraps me up.
     It wears on me.
       It hides my tries.
     It offers life.

It tries.

Only an Aeronaut Might Know

                          A translucent water balloon
                          alights from Nowhere's hand,
          drips,
                anchored by a metal stand.
It's attached to me,
      sinks its contents slowly
           underneath,
                inside my hook of elbow
    to a place where I can't see.

    Look, I'm not that stupid;
        I know it's an IV.
              But I'd rather it be ivy—
                  flowery, garish garland
        wrapped around my headboard,
            like to sleep with me is
the most "interesting" thing in the world,
      a celebratory fact
worthy of "beautiful" decoration.

            At the very least,
        I want to know
           what this kept concoction is.
            But they won't tell me.
            They catch me looking
                    and roll
            the stand around,
      till every word printed
on the zeppelin becomes
a secret message in espionage,

                    obscure,
      only known to those fluent
            in Mirror language.

        The Canadian One
saw me trying to make sense
of the hieroglyphs and told me,

        "Oh, don't you worry about that, honey."

Then she used a cloth knife to cut the room in two
and asked me if I wanted a spit tray and a cup of water
to rinse with after I brush.

                                I told her no,
                              I'll be alright.

I like the aftertaste of toothpaste
                still sitting on my teeth.
              After all,
                it reminds me:

                                I am clean.

Re-plugged, the Acoustic Version

I unplugged my heartstrings   from the machine.
    Beeping free.
        No metallurgy.
            No ghosts can detect me.

    I'm cool now.   I'm me.

    I waltz down the hallway gratuitously.
        I don't track the walk, but oft.

        I pee a lot.
            Just as much as I can.
    Some think I have a small bladder.
Others say I'm just bored.

This time, the release was well stored.
    Colored my vision burned black.   (Fell as it poured!)

    Split hands restamp circles,
        the clock echoes down the wall…
Fall bears the floater to crawl back, spinning silk to sew the pall…
    Roman legs and second eyes, two-four not eight-eight now…

    "What are you doing?
        These should never come undone at all…"

    Zero Room.   Full of hate.

Wow.

    My bed   is un-resting.

When they release me,   *I'm running*.

Too much gray   out my window.

Too much *high*   off the ground.

Phosphorous

"Oh, dear. You were dehydrated,"
                       Mary tells me.

                                    Hers is the face I rise to
              every waking day.
                  She says she's always with me,
                but I think she's only present
            for the platelet give and take.

She tears open a tiny paper bag
      of crude white sustenance,
         stirs the dose of dust in glass till it's beaten to oblivion,
         transforming tap water into a grapefruit taste.
I think I'm supposed to pretend it's hideous.
      But actually, it doesn't bother me.
         It may not be great,
      but it's still better than those smoothie things.
              And it's still nicer to me than Mary.
     I can tell she doesn't like me.
She reminds me of every substitute teacher I've ever had
      who told me I was dumb,
         asked me if I'd had a bad hair day when I took the test.
Every concert-less neighbor who yelled for me
      to *"Turn it down!"*
      reminded me Cobain's in peace,
      and they'd like to get some, so   *"Give it a rest!"*

              Jesus.

"Do you realize how serious your condition is?"

    "No."

      Truth be told,   I've never thought about it
      or questioned what bend of state I'm in.

"Yours are the lowest
blood phosphorous levels we've ever recorded
here in any human being."

    "So?"

        I guess I've always known.
        I leave half a drop left of a sip
        and set the cup down, hollow ring.

    She tells me,
"You've got to drink it dry. *Everything*."

        Oh, do I?
            Disgust.
                And the eyerolls.   *Clear.*
"Take better care of yourself
when you're out of here."

            Yeah.
                Sure.
                    Whatever
                        you like.
        I tell her, "I'll try."

                My dear.

    I'm not like the other kids here.
I'm a broken sewing machine who doesn't yet know
        how to sew up all these careful lies.

Always jagged zigzag,
        cheap resolve pull through,
rat's nest of tattered strings sleeping
                        underneath.

            I look to Olivine
                for all my answers
                      when Mary leaves

and The First and Second Woman
return to the room to speak to me.

They look all too similar, like One
must've rinsed her face in The Other's bathwater,
showered herself in the running hues of their features,
and decided to walk around like that for the rest of her life.
Or maybe they're twins.

They take a chair at my bedside,
ask me all about my feelings
and how long I've been thinking things so troubling.
I tell them since I was five years old.
They steal a sideways glance at one another,
closed mouth smile and stare into me
like I'm some kind of liar.

Do I have bugs crawling all over my face, or what?

"Five years old?"

It's not what they wanted to be told.
They wanted to hear it started last week,
when Little Johnny recoiled at the thought of taking
my manicured hand in his and failed to whisk me away
to Homecoming.

I try again.

"Okay, never mind. I lied. I was nine."

I remember being nine.
Sitting in the sandbox with my best friend at the time.
Worn pebble castles crashing back to dust
around our ashen knees,
as I told 'em my after-school plans.

"All my friends hate me. My best friend wants me to be dead. That's what she said. She left a letter in my mailbox once—five-handwritten-stapled-pages—and that's what it read. Lupine, she rhymes with witch. She caterwauls to the full moon in crescent sanity. Hell, we're—*nearly* all of us—adults here: She's-a-Dumb-Bitch-who's-gone-out-rockin'-on-her-high-horse-unicorn-broomstick. She-speaks-to-me-in-sentences-that-erase-themselves-like-lines-of-birdseed. Her-hair-tangles-in-zones-like-impatient-handwriting, like-the-script-of-a-lover-who-hungers-for-physicality. If she could find me she'd-eat-my-gingerbread-house-just-to-see-me-homeless, can-you-believe-it?! She meant to leave that letter for Someone Else to find, but she's-so-geographically-challenged-she-mistook-their-house-for-mine—and-I-don't-mind! 'Cause now they know all the lies she tells me to keep me barely breathin', and I know the Truth—how heathen!, how evil she can be! And is! Always! Not just when she's leavin'! Once, I-found-a-knife-on-the-floor in an abandoned room. It was smothered with the remnants of tart-berry-pie, the only kind she could consume. See, she's-always-imposing-these-feathery-limitations-upon-herself, Black-Lightness-only-knows-why. And no one has ever known that room before except her and I—I mean *me!* And I know what that knife was for: *to pirate me life!* So, I-took-it-with-me-and-I-shut-the-door-so-hard-I-let-it-hit-me-but-not-split-me-on-my-way-out."   !   !   !

They say I hop from one lily thought to the next like a frog.
They ask me if I think that's strange.
               No, not at all, I say.
   I can follow the way I arrange my everything's lost.
               Can't they?
They like not the order I sentence my structure
  nor minor the changes of a few lesser beauties for words.
They ask me if I always *almost* rhyme.
               I say no.
        Sometimes my words smith me silent.

             .   .   .
            In times like those, I pantomime.

"*Hmm.* Very interesting."

      Interesting
is one of the least interesting words on the planet.
Right up there with
     beautiful.

    Once, I tried to count the rings of Saturn
     with the blink of my robe-less eyelashes.
   I lost my way out there buoyed amongst the stars
      in sky's junkyard, kept Cronian ashes.

They write with fever in their notebooks.
I wish I could rip those secrets from their hands
  and hold them in my own.
    I wish I could make them forget how
      they move into me.
        The connection's sometimes fuzzy,
         though I found a sign again.
        Just as thin as what could never be
           mine to begin with.

      Arboreal acrobat,
  she's swung from these times before,
     at least a hundred dozen lines or more.

The zip-vine's slippery.
     Icy.
    But it sticks to me.
    Reads me.
       And beeps.
    Robotic predictability.
As though humankind itself were born
        from these machines.

What does she mean to me?
      Everything.
I adore our ritual of late night whispers
     where I steal right into her side
         of the tomb
    once they retrieve my body's
  chart of roadmap stickers.

"You mean the EKG?"

Yeah.
"Is that what the hell you call
that beeping thing?"

"Yeah.
You've never had one before?"

"No."

I'm not like the other kids here.
I might be broken,
        but I don't get sick   all the time.

Abasement for Rent

She tells me I'm a Strawberry Chick,
Martian green, cherry picked to fall,
enroll in this place,
hand ripen on the vine.
No sunlight will make it hard to comply—
but it can be done.
She's seen plenty of my kind
kick through to The Other Side.
But not *too* many.

"To be honest, you're kind of a rarity."

To be brutal, by that she means "freak."
But this cloth covers her and me.
Yeah, sure she's mostly cinnamon,
while Miss Allergy's black chocolate,
and The Greige One stays vanilla—
but over time these colors blend,
and tastes can change.

I've got my seeds on all my outsides,
fertile give in to my insides,
crescent hope there's fuller love
beneath my sleeves.

"We like a lot of the same things."

—Summer weather and when the rain snows,
—breadbasket rockers gettin' pissed at live shows,
—when they keep the ditched bridges,
—lyrics baritone-deep,
—elastic bracelets,
—wooden beads,
—and Halloween.

They found her secret high up in the trees.
Bags and bags,
she'd never been so low before.

Fatal heartbeat was the only warning sign they'd need—
and then it happened.

        Forty feet
             feels like a *pretty*
     l o n g

      fall

to   c   r   a   w   l .

But it could come
down
anywhere.

Still,

maybe we'd be better off
living life
a little closer
to the

g
r
o
u
n
d.

Those Nights You Gave to Me

She'd French braid her fingers into mine—one from the outside,
over, under—until where did one palm end and the other begin?
Our hands, tiny teacups steaming with detox promises,
hot peppermint possibilities.
Just her and me to the dining hall
 once I was strong enough to be wheeled in.

        My New Family—
       where do I begin?

    They seem like really nice people.
        Amongst them are:
—A Girl with the vision of silver screen.
     She smokes that charcoal eyeliner on *thick*.
—A Nationally Ranked Swimmer Guy
     who spends his days still out there, drifting underwater,
     lost eyes locked in space.
—A Boy who always keeps synthetic flowers tucked
     behind his ear. He's like, really cute,
     but perpetually not interested, ya know?
      and
—A Girl with a bleeding tongue
     whose wristband boasts a serious distaste
     for all island fruit.
         She likes Olivine.
          But not me.

          The Head brings a Face
      to stay with us every night.
    They each cast a careful eye on us,
      her and me and everybody,
        as we eat.
Sometimes it's Mary.
    Sometimes it's The First and Second Woman.
     Sometimes it's The Canadian One.

And sometimes it's Tom.

                Tom—
        where do I begin?

He has a mustache so thin
      sometimes I wonder
    if it's really there at all
or just a shadow of the man he wants
        to be when he grows up.
But he's like forty-three or four or five by now—
        not such a young pup.
That's enough nights gone by
    to act adult in life…
          am I right?

Is he alright?
      Am I?
Does he see what I see,
      when I see?
Or does he see more of me
      and not tell anybody?

If I really knew,
    could I still think of me
        the same?

Sometimes I wonder:
  What's in a name?

How He Likes to be Kissed

                The boy with daisies in his upkept hair
                    is very particular about his kisses.

The source must sparkle silver-less—
      no jewelry please.
Perfectly white teeth are most preferable,
but they can lay just as crooked as they like.
The duration of the first must outlast
      the obligatory stretch of accident,
            erase any mistake of possibility for regret—
                and end itself before the wave crests.

The lips should ask only easy questions,
      take nothing,
demand you receive the rush of self-assured emotions
swimming from one sea of open mouth
      to the unlocked sunken treasure chest of another.

Oh yeah, there can be open mouth.
                    But not *too* much.
There can be some uncharted detours.
                    But not *too* many.

There must still exist a mystery—
      an invitation to swim deeper
            into the island of a stranger,
a consensual truth
            that tongue has tasted only the beginning
                  of the most hallow trench of ocean.

And that's just the first kiss.
      Don't even get me started on the second.

Let's Not Talk About the Main Course

I lift

from the table—

more levitate   than meditate.

I leave the swell conversation

humming,

buzzing

on the ground,

a   wingless   bee—

more sociopath   than social butterfly.

Really don't want to partake

in what you're giving,

get honey-stuck in the jam

of   secret madness   un-jarred—

(some   call   it   gossip!)

One Day I'll Fly Again

I can't explain the rarity of rainstorms
    in these warmer months.
        Which is to say
maybe they're really not that rare at all,
    and the anomaly's another lie
we were taught to bow down to, led to believe.

                  God's always crying here.
                  Not me.
                  I don't know how to anymore.
                  I used to.
                  A lot.
                  All the time.

    People would ask me   "What's wrong?"
        when a shorter answer could be served to the
            question   "What's right?"
              (*Nothing.*)

Nothing is this stupid sky,
    always overcast,
        always sun at half-mast or passed out
            completely drunk again.

No birds are ever flown.
    No kites have ever known how to
        whip and kiss the earth goodbye—
            prayer-less wishes young children have
              wasted all their running on.

I envy them from above,
        who knows how many stories circling in the air,
        as they remove the lock from my vein.

I asked them to relieve me of this branding before,
    but they wouldn't listen.
        They said I might not be ready yet
            to exchange this hovered hissin' for free space.
Today, they changed their collective mind,
    founded a union of slaves to ungrave this silver sliver
        that's buried in me for so long
            it's claimed permanent residence,
    residual pieces of me   enveloping the abuse.

                        They tear and tear.
                        I won't tear.
                        I won't look.
        It's not about the hurt.
            It's not about what's better or worse.
            I just don't want to see
                who they're creating me into
                in the hook of my elbow.

                    I just want my window.
                    I just want this slate,
                this graphite,
            this lead pencil that never stays sharp,
that's always blunt as it's removed
                from this red,
                    blue line.

                I just want *you*,
                the old *me*,
                lost time
                out the glass,
                smoke,
        gone   mesh   screen,
                broken
as   you   restore me   to   being

                fine.

How to Engrave Your Life

"What's wrong?"

>Mary asks me
>as she enters the room.
>I edit the question in my mind.

"Nothing."

"Your 'nothing' seems so blue.
Maybe there's something you can sketch and share?"

>She's talking about art therapy.
>>It's our post-dinner group activity.

I'm fine with sketching,
>although I suck at it.
But I hate sharing.
>If I could just keep my feelings to myself
they could remain whatever color they're meant to be.
Add a presentation to the equation
>and everyone wants a front,
>earlier colors in the rainbow
>>that symboli(z)e a happier state of mind.

>>I've grown tired of pretending. And I don't think
>I'm much of an actress.

"I don't really think art's my thing."

>>*I remember a cool chick with tattoos once said*
>>*she hated drawing and had never made a memory*
>>*of any kind in her entire life.*
>>*She used shiny washers she found in the gutters*
>>*as beads to adorn the knots she collected*

in her dirty, dreadlocked hair.
She said she was allergic to bathbombs
and feared her pillow clouds would fall
down the shower drains.
Her sneezed droplets of spit came to raise a green garden,
sparkled like the afterglow of last night's
glittery eyeshadow, iridescence caked across her lids,
a frosty rainbow.

Mary elevates my wrist,
    prematurely presses two fingers
into its underside.

"Why don't you write?"

    "About what?"

    Her voice softens.

"A Wise One once told me to write what I know.
    The perfect thousand words can paint a picture
    far more precious and permanent
    than tempera could."

    She watches the secondhand on the wall
    give birth to a new o'clock.

    Not before adding:

"Give it a shot.
Write about your life.
Your best friend.
Your first love.
Write about *you*."

Paint yourself into a full ocean—
    a new body
     of salt water
        every day.
    A canvas of everlasting
          e x p e r i e n c e.   *(escape)*
    A collage of
    f r a c t a l s,
       words,
         imagination.
Borderless.
       Boundary-less.
Love
   both lost   and   found.
Friendships
   that have made a hometown
   of your open heart's   safe harbor.
     What the feeling would taste like
       if you allowed yourself to
    bend,
  break,
    lick the waves
      with your fingertips.

              Pulsing.
           Biting.
         Buzzing.
       Counting.
     Recording.
   Keeping
       —she scans my eyes for feeling—
all these vital signs

     of life.

Whore Story

My throat clears a cobweb of nerves
    I didn't know had bundled there
        until I tried to speak.
My words shiver in the clutch of my hands.
    I scan the horizon before me,
      view a sea of unwaving fans.
            This paper's weight is heavy.
            Am I still too airhead to properly sink?
It's been a while since I've relayed a Truth
    that spoke to me.
To anyone,
    let alone myself.
           Especially this urchin company.

"You're amongst friends,"
    Mary encourages me.

    She knows I've spent all day, my whole day
        creating this piece.

"Go on."

    She smiles.
    Her warmth is a lighthouse.

"*I'm amongst friends*,"
           I repeat inside.
"*All friends, no barriers.*"
                Ahem!
"*Like a coral reef,*
    I'm cool.
Like anemone,
    I know them."

I breathe in.
    I begin:

" Once upon a (miserable) time,
there were a whore.
(She talked however she liked
and Rebelled against The Laws of the English Language
for scarce a reason... but for a good time.)
She had a big, dumb heart who worked too hard
to love Everyone that hated her
and ugly eyes who kept seeing the opposite
in Everyone that called her "Easy."

Everyone vehemently denied her services,
but loved to remind her of her Title ("Whore!")
just as often as they possibly could.

Her best friend were a little whore, too.
She were allergic to mirrors and cheap perfume,
so she had to spray her disguise on in the dark,
hope it would stick.
She had a way of sucking
her brand-name lipstick until it pointed into the shape of a... well,
I'm-sure-you-can-guess-what.
She hadn't been invited to any raves in a while,
but she had a lot of too-tight crop tops
and padded bras
and clear platform heels
and fugly, white, lacy dresses
and black designer bags
that she really, really, really, really wanted to show off
just as soon as she possibly could!
A funeral seemed like an appropriate place
to don leopard print attire,
so she silently plotted her friend's suicide.
Yes, you heard that right...
silently.

You see, she were passive-aggressive.
Always passive-aggressive.
While her friend, The First Whore, well...
She were passive.
And then *aggressive.*
And then passive again.
And then aggressive like never before!
But never both at the same time.

And then there were this guy
who reminded The First Whore
of a flounder,
and he really, really, really, really wanted to use
and lose his V Card
but he carried no cash and were a racist dumbass
and once, he even cursed Kurt Cobain "overrated!"
!   !   !
So, The First Whore were like,
"Fuck outta here, dumbass!"
And the next day he told Everyone they "did it"
even when they didn't anyway!
And Everyone believed that fishy thing
what?, just because he had a ding-a-ling
and she didn't?,
so what could she say?!
And then, as if that weren't enough,
he stole an "I believe in mermaids" button
from The First Whore's backpack in history class
when he thought she couldn't see, too, behind her back
because her eyes only roll in the front of her skull.
Psh. I told you he were a dumbass!
And now the poor whore's been washed ashore ever since because
her magic fastens contagion
like her mythical venereal dis-ease
she don't have but Everyone wants to whine
"Ew" about anyway.
And it's all his fault.

And her stupid whore friend's fault, too,
because she probably put him up to the snarky tactic
in the first place.

So, until Death,
there's this:

The End "

And I exhale and see Mary,
        limbs akimbo,
    once magnificent eyebrows
drawn together in the crumbling black arches
        of an ornery mountaintop.

"I don't think that's a very nice story."

      Well, shit, neither do I!

"But I followed your advice!"

      What else could I write?!

Apology as Allergy

For some, sorry is a pineapple
sliced on the tip of their tongue—

heavy,
weighted,
stabbing,
acidic with the skin left on,
bleeding hurting juices
from the rind of thorns,
cutting,
blooming flowerless red
in the graveyard garden of their mouth—
yellow seeds of spent regrets,
silenced remorse for what Remedy needs,
wants,
wishes

but can't be said.

Art is Outlawed

Now we're not gonna have art therapy anymore,
    and instead

    we're gonna read inspirational quotes
    from the already torn pages
        of a four-year-old calendar
    and play b-o-r-e-d games
    and sit around in a handheld chain link circle
        after snack time
and share
        first our low point
                and then our high point
      of the day.

I'm   not   kidding.

                This lameness knows no end.

                And I'm just looking for a friend
                    I can blame this on.

Friendly Reminder

Suck it up, sit it out, shake it off, and take it.

You remind me.

    Some people are raped
        by serial monsters,
        by shadowy strangers,
        by hands familiar
        who once claimed to hold love.
    Some people get their throat slit from behind.
        Their head will never know a different kind
            of eye roll, no dull indifference, only death.
    Some people starve straight to death on accident.
    There are flies laying eggs in the open wounds
        that won't glue shut in the broken limbs
            of sick children in Africa.
And does anybody care?
            NO!

    There are metal crates filled with foxes
        who will be relieved of their jackets,
        electrocuted fully conscious,
        only fur left, the black thorn of an eyelash
            painted in red,
        as they blink into a short second half
            without skin.
And does anybody care?
            NO!

        Once, you saw a homeless man
      swim through a broken bottle of vodka
   because he made the mistake of taking a corner
         in front of a liquor store.

Once, I saw a woman open her car door
in the middle of rush hour
while she was stopped at a red light.
She threw up all over the street.
I was seven years old.
I still remember the color that came from her mouth.

I am just a Drama Queen,
a minor, depressive, seventeen,
a soft body full of middle fingers
who refuse to illegally fuck me.
A miser for misery
who blames her bullshit on the weather,
when I bought this blizzard!,
Iboughtthisblizzard!, IBOUGHTTHISBLIZZARDINMYHEAD!
Cut, breathe the high top from a mountain, then bitch,
"Oh, how it won't stop snowing!"
Cold, fast, crash down like a mirror,
then sit cross-legged on the floor in silent self-reflection
when there are plenty of unbroken IKEA chairs available.

It could be worse.
I could be dead.

I'm so blessed to have a vase full of stinking baby's breath
and cliché roses, all my least favorite color: red.

What would I do without you to remind me?!

We Got in Trouble

Everyone's asleep in this vicinity.
Not I, not I.

Not her, not me.

I'm too careful (not)
to wake the others here.
I'm never careful enough
when I need to be.

Always

I steal

away.

"Hey, think I can get a taste?"

She nods her head in the direction of my windowsill,
the heart-shaped lollipop left decorating the vase
of rose corpses, decaying thorns.

"It's all yours."

I rush back to her green eyes as nightlights,
wide awake "go" signs to give in to temptation.

"I want to show you something. It will be our little secret."

She tears the plastic from the sugar jewel
at a decibel more than she bargained for.
Grimace.
She brings the magic wand to her lips.

Her teeth are spaced so far apart
you could slip through them,
sweep the pink walls clean,
sleep in them
like little bunker gates of hell.

Her tongue swims,
a koi fish
across the candy pond,
baring the cold
glint of a brazen knife blade
like blown glass bubbles on the surface.

"No way. You have a tongue ring?"

Inner child of her smiles
the pain away.

"Yep."

"I had no idea."

She keeps it well hidden.

"That's what I like about it.
You'd never guess unless I gave you a hint
because I thought you could handle it, ya know?"

As if the jewelry kiss itself has roused her,
the divide unties, and Mary walks right up to me.

"What are you doing still awake? It's late."

It feels so early.
Electrical blackouts timed in sync to a metronome
come first

before the sun sets here.
"*You*,"
she says to me,
"need to be back in your side of the room."

She's firm this time.
No "dear."

I leave before I'm ready,
before I want to go.
I'm already over the wrist-slapping.
I'm already bridging the gaps
in our custom made
memory.

"We got in trouble,"

like spinning bottles at a sleepover,
my friend giggles endlessly behind the vertical sheet.
And I swear it ripples into life when I exhale
the wired breath it's built in me.

I turn under my blanket,
try to decide which side of me feels more centered,
more whole, or in need of deeper affection.
And for the first time since I've been here
I feel a little less alone.
A piece of me even thinks
her framework could begin to house my home.

Ain't that a funny thing?

I turn and I turn,
lit up in my wakefulness.

This kindled warmness,
there's no way to say thanks for this.

I keep my eyes open,
fixated on the ceiling.
Let 'em fall
across the opaque that quarantines us,
hanging in between
our separate yet shared
hurt turned laughter.

I whisper.

"Goodnight, Olivine."

Rest in Pieces Assured,
These Were Not Good Times

I am
the victim
of Grand Theft Auto Body.

They took my Olivine.

White partition tore, took life from me,
expelled the death of her "recovery"—
a wasted vacation of wasting time
and resources and too many requests to use the microwave
to heat things that were better off cold or in the bin.

What a hassle!
What a hard time!
What a sad reminder!

No, she didn't want a string of used beads
around her wrist
above a band professing her known allergies,
reminding her she was still here
and at the same time,
waving goodbye...
"Goodbye..."
She gave that strand to me.

He came to the room to bring her back home.
I'd never seen her cry the whole time
she roared into me.
I never thought the last time I saw her
she'd be silent and tearstained
in the arms of a strange man
I'd never met before.

But go figure.

They said she'd be back here in a week.

                                              And I wouldn't be.

I Have a Small Room with a Dead Fly in it

You give up
kicking
in your cracked robin's egg
blue

and it's no use:
I was too late.
You couldn't be saved.

Black needles collapse
inward
toward your stomach
like juice veins,
throw a tantrum
folded on your back
like stacked laundry
undressed
in Life's costume.

The curtain hides,
she's shy,
    she's shy.
It was no use.
    It was no use.

Filling Out

I know it isn't worth it,
but sometimes
I put pressure on the bruise
on purpose—
just when it begins
to fade from me
so I can
hold it for another while.

It keeps
all my memories.
Plus,
I like the shifty way
the shades bleed
the rainbow
in reverse.

Submerged.

I've always thought
purple was the prettiest,
the darkest color,
the deepest kiss.

Consensual…

And now I don't want to lose
that, too.

New Vacancy

They're finally ready for me
and now I'm late.
                        I've forgotten how
           uncomfortable it is to put on jeans,
              the intricate art form
             it takes to tie a shoelace.
          The placement of odd freckles
            Life collected for me,
       painted on the stretch of space
              about my ribcage.
    Washed up, "free" as beach glass bottles.
      Broken.   Didn't recognize the fallout
                as my own.
            Tried to brush mahogany
                                      away.

     "Congratulations,"
                    they say to me,
                       like my expulsion's something to celebrate.
      They'll never stethoscope the sound of my breath again
            if my life lays tracks according to their plan.
A measured drip of time in glass,
I've waited for this moment,
made that today would be it, the last,
    the end of me.
I never did have the means,
but now I hesitate to leave for a second reason:
        I don't want to go   back to everything I hated once,
            horizon-eye the days I wished
                    I'd never see.
No handshakes,
    only hugs here.
               I roulette my final rounds.

    "Goodbye..."

"It's been great getting to know you,"
    The First and Second Woman say.

"You're in my heart and prayers always,"
    Mary tells me.

"Don't see yourself back here,"
    Tom infantilizes, with
        (what I've come to believe is)
            a strictly platonic wink.

Two thick panels of glass introduce me to a narrow hallway.
    It shivers with pale, blue light.
    This river's winding.

    "Have a nice life,"
        The Canadian One says
            as she lets go of the open door,
                wishing I'll hold our bond forever,
                feel this closeness
                      as she clears me out.

        I step into the corridor,
            not sure which chamber of mine
                has been opened the most times,
                slammed shut the loudest.
                    Not sure how long the path
                        paves around aimlessly,
                  beating until beaten down,
              until it drums completely
                                    out.

No More Lonely in the Stables

Black tar has never stretched so brightly.
Strangers share halogen half-life of mine.
                        My deepest Empathy divides amongst
                            all the displaced, smile-erased, frown pushers;
They've never pollinated heartfelt soul,
    never peeled back the petals
        of this blossoming li(f)e.
Customers sigh impatiently in line at the drugstore,
    as the cashier overcharges them
            for birthday candles and matchsticks.
                I laugh (inside) and shake my head.
                    They just don't understand yet:
    This whole vast existence
        is one big, beautiful accident.
Nothing matters—non-depressing—nothing's important.
Every Adam's evolved at the quintessence of perfect timing
        to inhabit this world with me, in you, Eve,
                in the first footsteps landing on the surface
    beyond the front door—some say   "the moon."
My carpet's a little more familiar-stained
    than I've grown used to.
My ceiling's a little higher
    than I guessed the walls could climb.
Blacklight stars, plastic tacked above me,
        glow so close I could mistake their shine for mine.
        Un-sky-highed but smiling.
        Unkept.
        Returned to the stable of second chances.
        Unkempt.
        Undressed in friendly nothing
for the nightly eight-hour rest up for the next adventure.

        Damn.
                It feels surreal to be   a   l i (v) e .

Coffee, Cake, and Cigarettes

You feed me coffee and cake every day for breakfast.
You set my table with a cigarette and single rosebud
      yet to explode into maturity,
            open velvet in the ashes of my habit.

        I can consume poison next to something beautiful.
            I can find romance in a ritual.

      It works.
      For a little while.
But the accumulation of chemical compounds in the coffee
    leaves me wired (although I won't admit that),
    the fondant frosting never changes its color,
    and the cake loses its sweet taste.
    And like any good rose,
    soon enough all I'm left with is a face of erasure,
    a body of thorns,
    and a basin of muddied water
swirling with a stench that no longer folds itself inside
    the petals of a flower.

      I don't think this scene perceives depth anymore.
Don't act like this reprised warm-up can Champion my day.

    Like five,   I don't take snack breaks.
    I want my smokes not to break me,
      crack me,
    but to cataract my eyes blind to sight,
    birth   new   v i s i o n
so I can see something you would find worthy to be.

      Me.

      But different.

Everything   is the same awake.
So, when I sleep, I dream.
But it's not always pleasant things.
But it's always a scene I couldn't think of becoming.

Me.

But different.

Unbecoming.

But at least it's

Me

becoming someone   unwrapping routine,

rearranged.

At least it's different.

Me.

Becoming me.

Green Turquoise

I'm cleared to return,
    be brought back to books with thick spines
        and such leathery hardware.
            Metal desks that quake dizzy from a ghost's touch.
Learn.

    At school again.

        My heart's no longer at risk
        of attacking itself.
    I can synchronize the uniform of neutrals
    hanging in my closet instead of me,
      in place of the syncope
they no longer fear I'll fall victim to at random.
        I'm free. I guess.
        Or whatever.

    I'm not as happy as I think I should be.

            Shouldn't I be a little more… *hippie?*

Don't they expect me to come back tan, in sandals
and hemp rope belts swaying around my cello hips,
with newly formed callouses still soft on my fingertips
    from finally having enough centered patience
      to properly pick up playing guitar?
I'm supposed to evoke a crisp whisper of clarity.
Eff off all the excessive curse words, of course.
Ever so slightly avert my gaze to the Heavens
    when I speak of "Spiritual Things."
    Walk down the hallway smiling
        for no reason.

I will let the whole world down ungently,
honey free, to crash from lunar flight.
Or at least everyone involved in my own.
I will. I think. I might.

The sink beckons me sideways.
Twisted dark hair offers two (more or less) even sections;
I take what's underneath,
eager to create an effect, a mermaid aesthetic.
I swim bleach in generous handfuls
from the nape of my neck to the deep-fried ends
of split black threads.
I leave the magic potion on too long.
On purpose.
It's gotta be worth it,
as starkly close to white as I can get it
for what I'll color it next:

Turquoise.

Ocean waves cascading across my shoulder blades…
That's what I envision.
I'm gifted another version from the experiment:
a troubled sea as green as my inexperience
in creating myself a Beautiful Thing worth loving.

I need to dye
   it all
back to black,
   but first
to yellow
   again.

Sigh tumbles like a sunken ship.
No sailor wants to come for her.

Because you haven't had a complete mental breakdown
until you've effectively effed up your hair, right?

So now I can check that off the list.

I need a bucket.
And a mop.
I've splashed freckles of the rainbow
all over the bathroom floor.

Seriously Serrated

It was an accident,
I swear.

She tells me she's so happy
it's a knife cut   and not a cat scratch.
Those wounds bury   deep and dirty,
flare infection   like a hair trigger.

She doesn't sew me up.
She glues me shut
with butterfly tape—
dust-free medicinal wing.
Clearly   the next big medical thing.
Translucent.   I never knew what she meant until I met you.

I get called "Whore"   by a Bitch   I've never met before
as I'm talking to you.
You tell her to
"Hey, be nice."
But she's already gone
when the request has left
your mouth.

I kissed it once.
For eight seconds.
First, I saw no one was there.
I kept my eyes closed.
Did you open yours?

I lie,
"It doesn't hurt."

I pretend   I never heard her voodoo stare
as I silence the redness   burning up my swallowed verbs.

Life After the First Place

I go over to my slut friend's house.
        If you can believe it,
   I think even less people love her
               than they do me.
   But she also gets label-whipped
   less with the verbal pistols,
       so I guess it's all worth it.

"It *is* worth it!"
        she tells me
        of the five-finger discount display
             she ransacked, left ramshackle,
          the straight-off-the-runway
              bags and shoes and bad moods
and long/sad whore-sy faces she practices
             blowing kisses with, frowning
                 into an open compact.
                 So closed off.
                       Sad and long,
                           so sad for *so* long.
"It's *so* worth it!"
        "And you deserve it..."
                 a gone guy to buy you nice things.
             Because that's my purpose, right?,
                 as a friend to remind her
             how much she flatters us all
                     with her being.
       This high-end, this fashion plate,
   Miss—Damn it.
       Her dad's home late.
            Or wait—
                 is he early?
Early.
  Hardly nine-thirty on a Sunday.

Wasn't expecting him till Thursday.

He stumbles
    to keep from sitting at the stand of me.

"Wow! I almost didn't recognize you.
    You've really gained all your weight back!"
            "I've really gotten quite fat now,
                haven't I?"
"No, no. Not *fat*.
    More like… *curvy*.
    Have you been eating
        like crazy?"
            He asks me all about
                The First Place
        and what they did to me there.
How crazy of me to think we could talk about other things.
        His new workout regimen.
            His new twenty-six-year-old girlfriend.
            This expensive French press
        that brews coffee beans.
    Only the freshest,
        only the finest cups of joe
            at his breakfast table.
    No room for the silverware
        of second best there.

    Mourning's re-entrance to the Lair blares a glaring quiet.
Sister scowls at me.
    I wore pants today.
    Today's a skirt day.
Where's my khaki gown?
        Apparently, God wants to ogle my thighs and shins.
            He teaches religion
                every period
    and waits at the bottom of the staircase

                as we climb,
                        hidden,
                                celibate in sight.
                        Yeah.
                                Right.

"But I can't wear a skirt today.
        My limbs should limp
                with a trigger warning!
        I've got third degree memories
                                all over my skin."

The advice I'm given?

"Oh, bless your heart, dear.
    Come with me.
I've got the perfect thing."

                                Tattered maxi rag that licks
                the dusty ground of scattered bruises
                                rummaged
                        from the musty lost and found.
        Oversized fabric of a million other
                        Faceless Nameless
swallowing the shape of me.
        Fate calls the way this desert frown hangs "Happy."

In religion class
        I'm forced to discuss politics
                with a guy I've never talked to before.
                        I think he'll Holy hate me
                when we don't believe
                        in the same candidate for president.
But instead he shows me his
        wish-crafted scenery from noble dreams,
                all the goals in global reach he hopes will be achieved

                        for the whole world (ending)
                in the next four years.
    He smiles
            when he shakes my hand.
He tells me
            it was "nice" to meet me
                        when our conversation leaves.
        Maybe the path to peace
            is less winding than it seems.

A guy who once told me
        to go eff myself
                for reasons that are still obscure
tells me he likes my sweater.
        It's the ugliest thing I've ever worn—
                and in this skirt, that's saying something.
                        But it's soft. It keeps me warm.
            (It still holds the witch hazel of his aftershave.)
I don't think he was lying.

The teacher who once slammed
        a door in my face
                before the bell chimed
                        because I was already late
        invites me with a Cheshire smile
        to enter the room... *tardy.*
Then the guy front row center,
        he gets kicked from his seat because
"There are people out there
        who need a chair more than you do.
We all must covet patience, learn to share."

The girl whose locker opens
        next to mine
                has steel eyes now.

When they see me
        they ask quiet questions
    I don't really feel like answering.
       Not because I like secrets,
but because I found out,
        only recently,
   I can't lie.

      I see this chick
        whose name sounds better
in its masculine form.
       She uses a false falsetto
           that cracks,
     betrays her level of ease
         to speak to me.
She tells me she likes my hair.
      That's what her words say,
but her soul conveys:
     I thought your heart was gonna contract its last
        expansion—no arterial building upon another day.
Either way,
the response it elicits from me
should be the same.
    And it is.
I remember everything
  I've ever learned about friendship,
      and I tell her,
"Bitch, please.
   You and I both know
it didn't go
as I'd planned."
          Her eyes hold mine.
          Her hands hold my shoulders.
        She hugs me.
            "No, really. I like it."

Whore.

I say I can't go back to school anymore.
I fucking hate that place.

"Were people mean?"

"No, they were nice to me.
    Too nice.
It was uncomfortable."

    See—
        I don't want to cry
            at home to the memory
        of those sad storage eyes
            and all the too-late apologies
                from aqua guys
            and all the well-wishes
                from infallible strangers
                    that remain better off
                          unsaid.
        I want to get out!
            And never come back!
                I want to LIVE a life
                I can leave.
                I want to be…
                Somewhere
                I can
                find me.

They warn me not to run.
Running will make me stagnant.
Stagnation will make me (more) arrogant,
    careless,
    retrograde
        into the old ways.

  I do what I want anyway.
      I always do.
I could care less.
      I move.
            I fly
                  sky high away
                        to another life,
                              another land.
                                  Another man.
                                      First class,
          I never do catch his name,
but I'm sure I'd recognize
                  his giving hand.
    I have a two week [faux-]mance
        with a Danish flight attendant.

"I see you everywhere,"
                  he says to me.

            Well that's true.
                Over Ontario,
                    Greenland,
                          Iceland…
        and back "home,"
to *his* homeland,
        and home base again.
    Basically,
        everywhere *we* go
we *both* go.
                    I romance him—*hard!*—in my head
every day for a fortnight—
                      and that's all the love I need.

I sing
     in languages I can hardly speak.
I listen

      to rap music in Finnish
and get lost in *the rhythm,*
    the rhythm,
       mm-mm-
    the-rhythm.
          I-love-the-music-for-the-vocals-and-the-beat.
Sonja from Helsinki tells me,
      "Don't understand this in wrong way,"
and Elvis from Riga
        -by-way-of-St.-Petersburg-
          (but-*shhh!*-
            it's-a-secret-for-some-reason-
              haven't-you-heard?!) says,
"To be honestly…
    Did you know
as well as Nirvana…
there's Mudhoney?"

          And believe me when I say,
      "to be honestly,"
    it's no shade on Kurt Cobain…
      just a ray of sun to the underground, hun!
        This band…
          I can't get enough!

My tribe, my life…
    What have I found?
      What have we done?
        It's so fun
      to be out.

        I don't think
        I'm e v e r gonna
        come back down
          a g a i n .

The One About the Body and the Bee

My heart's more hear
for a song your Hands never played for me
than Machine Head will ever bee
in plurality,
buzzing like a symphony
of orchestrated Soul.

For they, too, know the pistol,
ride the piston behind some
Black Velvet banner of Violet wings,
violent eighties bridges,
nineties unplugged guitar strings,
and some other things (un)forgot,
(un)pollinated—

"Hated it!"
        "So much they made and mated it?"
"Yeah, *that's* how much they hated it!"

Freely refused to stay inside,
the stamina silently mourns the unborn
Live, like the Freefall of
something that was—
Nevermind,
Never Said to begin with   at all.

This hard Rock body of (un)Love   lost.
Generation g o n e.

Red in the sink.
Blood on the Ground.
Leaky faucet   for the flower   Blooms
unfound.

See dust out.

You Used to Teach Enlightenment

I met a Spiritual Goddess
on a beach   in the South of France.
I saw her praying on the rocks   under starlight
to a Clear Spirit   just past midnight.
    Folded petals of a lotus flower   blooming,
       breaking open,
        waiting for a come up   to crash down,
rain absinthe embers
of enlightened emerald sound.
    Omnipresent,
        Eco-conscious—

              What am I doing still awake?
                    It's late.

            The day's sun cyclops eye
       has shuffled shut its silken fan of lashes,
         has surrendered to weeping willow,
                  Angelica,
                  nightshade,
         and so now, must I…

Unspoken display,
  statuesque,
Adonis
    resting   beyond this mountaintop,
    the haunted   double staircase   view…

                   Sometimes I jump.
                   Sometimes I think
                   this time I'll fly.

Life begins
Underwater
with you.

Not No, Yes

She used to run her angel food
through vodka
    just to smoke a sponge
    filtering your Spirit.
        That's what she told me.
        That's what I believe.

She's still flighty, but not in origami airplanes of the sea
    or opaque bottles, cursive messages…
        Rubberneck in glass,
        crash,
        cast the casket,
        prep the eulogy—

No.

    'Cause of course, to write the words,
      someone's heartstring highway
      would have to bleed
        the pulp of sacrificial seed.
      No toxins filtered by the rise of bread.

Those days have left both her and me.
        Buried.
        Dead.

No.

    She gets distracted often, yet in innocence.
        Loses her footing
    in that hazy REM stage fading.
    Trips on her shoelace.
    Forgets what she's just said.

When I first spied, I heard her recite
a Norwegian poem in a tongue so broken
even I could tell it was not her native one.
But Norse language is fun.
That's what she travels for.
She loves Terrebonne, the Caribbean, Cusco,
Tokyo, Queensland, Budapest,
Sierra Leone, Rome,
Dublin, and Berlin.

We call her Nine.

Yes.
Not "No,"
but "Nine."

But why?

"It's the Number of Change in Numerology."

Ahh, Divine.

Namaste.

All day
listening to her
unlock the lore of healing crystals
in a lesson, not of chalkboard
but of chakra.
Not of three ring binders
but of rings on every finger.
They bind us together by green,
a calm mood seen by the emotion hue of the band.
(If you don't know what you're feeling,
check in with your hand.)

                    Every time I spin around I think I may throw up.
                                      In swivel chairs.
                                              Standing.
                                              In midair.
                                      Even underwater.
Once,   I thought the sun would save me
                              if I danced myself into the sea.
                                        I was wrong.

          When I wash the salt remnants of a slow burn
                    I learned in earnest
                    from my skin
               for what could be the last time this time,
              I hope I'll be a little more like Nine.
That's how I'd do it   right.

                        But I figure I'll always be
                        infinitely swirling
        into something a little more
                            like eight.

     The knife-st part is flesh uncut,   a l i v e .

                      That lesser way's
                            more   mine.

I Am Not a Marionette

She says
    I need to s e v e r
        the s t r i n g s that slave
        my s o u l.

    I can no longer search   for me
    in feelings,   in loving memory,
    in the nostalgia   of wishful fairy seeds.

I am not broken things,
        the appearance of me.

                Cerulean vine,
        a silver weight   determined by the way
             of Someone Else.

I am not dry drowning   or   roarless screaming.

I am not a swailing   started from snapped matchsticks,

a crisis
    only when the compound corridors smith darkness
                from my waning light.

I am not a me   of two parts,
a survival   and   a greater good.
        I am not good.
      Or bad.

Revamped mistakes   or   ones worth making.

I am making me,
        through lines already
                mine
                    and
                    tethered.

I float,

                unsinking
                        anchors
                                land

                        back   home,

                                        becoming   free.

Only Me

I don't know what happened.
I thought I'd wake up
to the swell of your soul singing,
a tangle of your whisper kisses
enveloping me like a letter
I'd already licked the clothes off
and dismissed to write.

But you're not here.
And you left me
a l o n e
in this night-stained sky.

I don't remember
your dreams.

Tumbling instruments of sound
still play
on repeat.
Elevator music,
background noise.

But not a canopy
for your voice.

Cali-King size
twin beds are not enough
Holy mattress
to blanket
the unrest I feel.

And disappointment.
Loss.
Unfound.

Extra Spectral Display of Confetti

I float
the box ashore from 'neath the sink.
Faded, folded photographs.
Black and white ultrasound,
violet cradle to azure earth.
Rose plays, piano keys.
Kindergarten, some late teen series circle
'round a rectangle table.
Cakes with candles, fire wick flames.

(Each breath bends a distant name.)

And some of them are *you*.
And some of them are *he, she, they*.
And some of them are *us*.
And all of them are *me*.
Not to stay.

Only Some Significant Other

can light write my image through a lens of nonexistent hue,
archaic interfusion of a primal blend.
I will not lend myself to the ageless painting
of false beings any longer.
I will not see me in ol' factory productions ceased,
or otherwise ramshackle sense astray.

Three cones of   creation,   "colors"
colliding, hallucination
of a me not me from some   "back then."
(Not where I'm going to now, no.)

I scissor my static self to smithereens.
    Craft confetti from the planes of my face.

      Eyeballs and smiles,   *eyeballs and smiles.*

            What did I ever need them for?
            They're just things after all.

    Let 'em rain,   let 'em fall

        free,   cut my hand.

      Shore, see me standing.

   My skin bleeds halide memories
        on the linoleum floor.

  I surf my plumaged crest
to feather dust the outskirts no more.

For

What did I do that for?

> Destroy the visual record of my existence
>   on the bathroom floor
>   all but simultaneously,
>   as I locked my entrance
>   behind the door.
> Couldn't there be something else
> I wanted more?

Oh, I don't know.
              A nap?
                              A moment's quiet reflection?

Hmm.
    Now that you mention it,

                      no.

Those things now don't speak for me.
                        And speaking of me:

> Now I have a foreign accent
> rolling across the tip of my tongue,
>   a voice I've never used before.
>   I've made myself
>   less *mundane folk,*
>   more *mythic lore.*

      A soar
          of metal wings returning orbit
                routes to unearthed land
  propel pronunciation properly from my lips—
but it's scoffingly stuffy.
  No one enunciates like this anymore.

Royally,
          I'm a little strange.
                  A little stranger in between
     the   violet,   scarlet   spectral wheel.

        Orange peel of passion, citrus fruit
           pucker to kiss the underneath,
              heal the ugly wounds past flesh.

        I did my best to address the friend
        robe's never known beyond still life
        depictions of solar times.
   Her soul or mine
                  should be freed now
                          to climb   o u t

                my window
                      forevermore.

What did I do that for?

Free Will to Follow

They motivate me with their speech,
        send wiry barred guys to my bedroom
                to talk sense into me.
Pinstriped collared shirts,
    pleated dress pants—not jeans.
Glasses so thin
    I can't believe   they aid in vision.

They tell me all about   glistening crystals,
    all the verbs they used to do to them,
            and—*Yeehaw!*—
    but now they love wearing them
        and instant coffee, see?
    Moonstones feast on fight-less knuckles,
        Amethysts grace the olive branch of neck
           —decaf after three PM, of course—
           And   *—hot damn!—*
    This life right here,
  it could be so sweet.
           So sweet.
        Sweeter than artificial sweetener,
    which is to say hundreds of thousands of times
           sweeter than actual sugar.
    This life right here,
  it could be the real deal—
      or dealings of the devil
               dealing me in.
  But either way it's my will,
                 ain't it?

  So do what you will.
        But make the right choice.   Or else.
           You'll be nevermore forevermore.
              Or at the very least, forever ill.

Miss Unwonderful

Mr. Wonderful is not

>gonna prostitute himself
>at some brain freeze of a job
>just to thaw at home
>(still not warm enough to face *your* face)
>and trip on your excuse of bullshit
>dribbling as to why you can't get out of bed.

>It's nine past five past nine
>on the sixth day of the week.
>The floor can't find you
>under all those magazine clippings,
>rejected clothes, carpet pillows.

Mr. Wonderful is not

>gonna appreciate yer fuckin' mouth.
>Spittin' shit like that depreciates a Dumb Bitch,
>Gaw-damn it.
>It's heinous. It's uninviting.
>An' all that frown shit? It ain't allowed.

Mr. Wonderful is not

>gonna brush the tangles in your hair
>and rip 'em out.
>That's *your* calling.
>Answer the phone.
>Tell 'em it's you.
>Ask 'em, "How are you?"
>Listen.
>Chew.

>. . .

        Don't talk with your mouth full,
                that's rude.

Mr. Wonderful is not

        gonna want some Shaky Hand
       too afraid of its own penmanship
     to scrawl black eyeliner on straight,
       too unattached to its own body
      who can't hold still long enough
to upward swing red love songs written in lipstick.
          I mean, look at you,
     you sloppy, stumblin' sideways bitch.
              I mean,
         are you even *trying*
        not to break mirrors?

         Seven Years bad luck,
just like the Seventh Year's lost itch.

           You've lost it.

        You might as well find

             nothing.

A Bachelor of Crude Arts.
    A Master of   A s y m m e t r y .

On Losing Friends

They're still allowed   to smoke
         thin vanilla cigarettes at the pink shed
   and fill water bottles with Clear stolen secrets
         and hopScotch a breakfast of battered "eggs"
    if last night's dinner was "frosting"
            and dessert was "milk and cookies…"
And invent and use stupid codenames for hot guys,
    illicit (de)vices that saw us through The Stone Times.
          And keep Alyssum-lined shrines of The Fantasy
   in that forbidden corner of the convent
         pent-up like a moan.

Now I sit in noninclusionary isolation of conventional exclusion.
             Off limits. Out of line.

                 Alone.

They say the "it"ness of my factor's been badly hacked
   by badder adverbs, ipso facto, I'm Holy
   expulsion out of Ice, Enlightened Mind.

I just don't think I have much   in common with them
                                       anymore.

     Plus,   I've tried to ring them
                 before.
     All   I got was a dial tone.

Ditched for Glitter in the Gutter

My best friend keeps leaving me for a needle.
        She's an Alien.
              Venusian Space Babe.
                      Cross Country Grunge Goddess.
        She keeps running away,
                chasing more north-stained s tar s.
        Her rapid footprints are flown black
                      little concrete soles.

I threw away my shoes,
        let my barefoot body break the life
              of full-length hanging
                      right in front of glass.
    Spiderwebbed my image,
        the mosaic aftermath of
Westward Moor.
    I didn't bleed.

Alas,

        I took a shot
            and thought I got 'em all.
        I left one
            stealing away
            the lie
                of you-and-I
            together.

Whatever.

            The one unframed
                has worn colorless soft,
                      faded at the edges
              of a memory   I keep tracing

                with an orchid kiss,
            pressing into your flash imprint
                        waiting for more truth to flow.
    But it never does.
        And if it did,
            I'd probably drink that, too.

Alone in this room where there should be you.

        The candle melts,
            wax rains in a pool.

To think!,
            I used to weave my fingers through the flame!
                She taught me that game!
    To run with fever heartbeats from the warning signs,
        take no chances slowly,
                    say the worst of yours were mine.

                Guess she never thought
                she'd run out of giving.
                Guess I never thought
                she'd get caught in the site.

            Early AM, but let's call it late night.
        I see with noon dimension
                    on the wall,
                            all these shadows cast—

                ugly,
            masquerading light.

Speaking of a Masquerade...

I try to manifest
    my cell number
        straight into your stem of brain,
            spiraling vine birthing light
                to a flower in bloom.
      Petals of pressed digits
          on a plastic device...
                Nice, nice.
      Okay, close your eyes.
          Slam them shut!,
      Think harder, *harder!*
              Not *too* hard.
      After all, I'm a delicate flower.
              But not *too* delicate.
      After all, I'm still the baddest bitch
                you'll ever know.
Hey, check it: Remember when
    we'd get a rise reciting lies
of those we'd known
              in The Biblical Sense?
But those lists were hit or miss...
      like, always miss and never hit,
          but sometimes wanting it, you know?
    Like those prospects were the gospel...
      Oh wait, oh fuck. Oh, never mind.
Alright, alright.
    Are we getting somewhere?
        There are only seven words
           you need to know.
    Or maybe more if you've flown
              on to better things.
    Let's say you haven't,
        for my sake, at least.
            Because that would leave me (more)

                alone in my misery.
Yes, I know what they say about company,
        how you should always pour your guests a drink.
                But I wish tap water ran like vodka
      overflowing from the sink.
And yeah, I used to keep a bottle (empty)
                      tucked (bedside) beside a memory.
      I can't help that I got thirsty.
            Like, are you even trying to remember me?!
Okay, I know, I know.
      You'll need one before the area code.
But maybe take two in case
      the first one breaks its way to your lips
                    or something tragic.
The other half of the mask
    is kinda manic.
            Mechanical rounds and dips of frown lines,
                  rings as planetary standbys
        for a matrimony waiting on a mattress
            just unboxed this spring.

              I fall.

        Gawd damn, it's everything.
        All at once it's happening—
this nothing, it sounds, slaved in me,
obliterating as only nothing could.

        I can't pick myself up.
    I'd tell you to leave a message—
        if you ever get there.
But I don't have an answering machine.

Gawd damn it.
        See what I mean?

No, She Hasn't

                              I don't pick up on the first ring
                                           or the second.
                                  The phone is in my hands,
                          but she doesn't need to know that.
              I whisper before the last chance to speak
                                          comes and goes.

          "Hello?"
"Hey."
          "Hey."

          .   .   .
"Well…?"
          ?   ?   ?
"I've been trying to reach you for what feels like forever."

                                                    No, she hasn't.

                                      I haven't left this room.
                  I've stared at the same wall without blinking
                          for seventy-two hours, unending.
            I've counted four thousand nine hundred
        and thirty-four individually raised stucco sections,
          of which over four thousand nine hundred
                    held the imprint of her fist,
                    the boundaries of her jawline,
                    the likeness of her silhouette.

    "*You've* been trying to reach *me*? *Pfft*. That's funny."
"Oh yeah? And how so?"

                                             This Dumb Bitch.
                She once called me the mother effing "C" word
                just because I refused to run away with her,
                            take refuge in her bed—
                even after I told her I didn't feel well,
                                I'd had enough,

and in fact,
had just been pronounced clinically dead.

The quake begins in spite of me. My hands,
two bodies of unbridled excitement turned bad,
too mad to hold the glass of Gone without shaking, stirring,
spilling my contents on eroded, rocky surface,
vehemently lifting, leaving—*No!—I can't do this!*
It was never supposed to be stung free, so useless, to end this way.

Hate when I'm like this. Meaningful-motionless.
My airways, an open portal to the landfill
of decay inside. Uncontained, all these stale thoughts
rush a geyser hydrant right out my mouth.
I can't be quelled,
can't be slowed down.   *Hush!*
The truth pours fast, brash, brave
and *LOUD!*

"You know what?
Why don't you just *fuck off*. I'm *done* with you."
"Excuse me?"
"You heard me: *Fuck. You.*"

And it's too bad I've just cursed into my cell
because I desperately want to slam
the receiver down with finality.
I hang up.
She calls right back.
I answer.
She says,
"And by the way bitch, just so we're clear:
I've been listening to Mudhoney
before you even knew who the *fuck* they were. *Bye.*"

No, she hasn't.

Sender Bender

I've tried and tried and tried
            to tie this friendship knot,
        secure these wooden beads in place.
This bracelet has been worn so many nights,
    the inscriptions have smoothed themselves over,
the clear elastic has stretched for what could be
            the very last time.

            I've tried and tried and tried
        to snap my fingers back in place with you.
I removed the memory of my face—but not yours.
    I left my mattress in an abandoned building
                I walked to.
        I crawled home
    and slept on the floors
        of my bedroom,
            kitchen,
                        basement...

            You
        have left
    such an unquenchable
            well
            in me.

        Hungry
    for penny wishes,
        the belief
    that magic travels
from your mind to mine
through a series of channels
        intertwined,
            ivy,
        static-free.

I have written you.

I have bubble-wrapped my sentiments in plastic,
sacrificed them to the seas.

I've waited and waited and waited
like a stamp in your right-hand corner,
like a backspace bar you won't return to.

"Maybe there's a problem
with the way that I phrase things,"
Someone Else once said to me.

"No, it's not that.
I used a language only you and I spoke."

I said that.

"I don't know what it is."

Just *please,* write back.

Desserts in Europe

Welsh a little Dutch of tongue
over your Friesland,
    Greenland—

    Hungary...

Italian surprised
    at your Russian Finnish!
        Flemish,
            but so Swedish,
        this Iceland.

Portuguese,
    Ukraine Spain
        to the Great isles of Britain?

Irish I could
    French you now...
    Greek Danish Netherlands
        Norway...

Welsh,
    Czech this!:

And I just want you!,
to French so hard I can taste
the German comin' out your mouth...

        Surprised at your fluency
                (or maybe my own?!)
        Little bumps of tongue
           soufflé across
    a mushroom cloud
of sound.

I See Stars in the Sink

She washed away
the starlight of last night,
the dirty hope that
you, too, weren't a wish
to shine for only a moment,
then burnout, dust fallout
in the empty place
of a happened handshake.
        Wanting more can't replace
        a stellar recollection
        she can't erase.
She washed you away...

            Light liquid soap
          promised rose petal,
            nightshade,
           antibacterial—

            But what if I wanted your germs?
            What if I'd drink Your Seed
            from the prefab floor of lies
            you just stepped on,
            like a bird, like a bitch?
            Like the warm water burns soft,
            cold locks the blood in the cloth,
            stains the scars ungone—
            Like I still don't see stars in the sink,
            down the drain!
            Like a *Need*
            in the cage of your ribs,
            fuckin' hold me.
            I am lonely.
            And now I am clean.
            I washed you away.

Is This Where I Quote Nietzsche?

The End,

     free
by your admission,
is something I can sink into.
         Hence the open invitation
         of the phrase "in the end."

At the end,
        I want not to be
    reduced down to nothing
    but to be
    built up into something
      created,
          as if for the first time,
             beyond "just" a memory.

I want to fully exist,
    handcrafted in your mind,
         forever molding into someone
I can only be
    in the allowance
    of your experience
      and its decided ambits
    of this limitlessness.
      Sinking like soldered metal
         smithed into existence—
different,   new
    every time you
      tinker with me,
        refine in your drumline of a heart
          the undertones of symbols chose,
    clash   the cadence of the voice
      I used to speak to you.

With words
and phrases so ambiguous
I think Nietzsche himself
might rise from the abyss
to stare into me,
waiting for the right answers to blaze
a certain flame of knowing sparked from violence,
pressing erasure so hard
into my skin I break the end of my damn pencil
to begin with when they don't...
Stop filling blue lines of college-ruled notebooks
beyond red marginal breaking points,
mending metaphors
of the written form and me,
as I wonder in loud silence:

What if this is all

just a vast

waste

of

time?

Would I even be

sorry?

Sit and Wait

I just sit
        in parking lots
             waiting for you
      to move
          with purpose
                    from the glass doors
                of storefronts—
automatic
      in automobiles.

I just wait
      for the names
              to stop!—
get to mine,
      hurry up.
             Don't want my voice
                  to break
      its way
                        to your ear.

I just sit
      by myself at noon,
          not high enough,
    and there's not enough
        comfort in cake
        (I don't want
           anyway)
        that could ever
           replace
        the missed taste
                of you
    on my tongue, on my breath
    in this
  weight,   here.

Seeds of Soul

She ascends the stairs
    like she's been here before.
                      Easy.
    Finds her way around
       the kitchen.
Has spelled her name with pasta
    in broth the same color as blood
                but more viscous.

The thickness of this past life sticks
              to her,
the one with caramel skin and salt wave hair.
    She cries for no reason.
    Simple things amuse her.
       She gets by on crescent fortune.
    She gets high on love and laughter.
And when I say "high,"
    I mean sky sweeps the floorboards
              of her porcelain ceiling.

              She forgot what pain meant.
    She forgot the difference between us
              was displacement.

            I tried to call her once.
                She didn't pick up.
    She could never erase all the space
              that stays between us,
tracking the Eros of an eighteenth orbit in marrow
    like trees. As if I could ever forget the wish I made
to know her better than this place on Earth,
       the words she wrote, her worth,
and how our time remembers her.

Your Hand

sky dances to a cappella symphonies
rolls in rhyme schemes like fairy seeds
coasts
is better off for it
knows you're better off for it
offered you a mountain view
to appreciate the good in everyone else's
bedroom window
blue like birthday candle wishes and paintbrushes
years stretched like a canvas of islands
you could dust us in
stars shooting like the Moon Goddess you gelled us in
acrylic sentiment
forever
by ingredients flowing freely from your fingertips forever
spice cake secret wishes home could be forever
lost in this surf city drifting country
twisting hanging undressing undulating like a dolphin
like a childhood
like an urchin to the melody
private concert of string and sand
only your hand can play in harmony—
only your hand can understand

As Once, So Forever

There's this lady-chick
    I see all the time,
        but I've lost my voice
            to speak to her now.
    Call it "selective laryngitis,"
        selected by a Larynx Master not my own.
    And now
        every time I see her
            I have to pretend I don't.
    Can't make it more awkward
        trying
        than it has to be, you know?

You see,
    I had a dream
    I fucked her husband,
        and now I feel so guilty…
  because I don't…
    feel undeserving…
        of this affair,
    ("don't-call-it-that")
            affection,
    this piercing,
        this bullet,
            this attention,
    this tongue ring,
        this better-than-a-cat-call,
    this connection…

not in my unconscious
        false reality
    or now.

Especially not now.

To be a hushed, kept secret
        has conceived in me
a Renaissance,
        pearlescent lens of dirty thoughts,
            brand new ones
        I have never known before.

Does that make me a whore?
    No.   I don't think so.
    Or maybe.   Hell, if I know!
        The difference made by primal scenes
            means I don't care anymore.

Now I have to pretend he's not beautiful, no interest piqued,
            like I hadn't stayed a little too much on him.
        Like that bed didn't know rock, roll, and rhythm,
            whole day staying in stamina.
            Like the headboard wasn't pistil-
            wrapped with purple pollination.
                Like that wasn't the first time
            my skin knew the blade of a knife
                    that couldn't cut me.
    And like he wasn't loving me, too,
        in my imagination.

    Because that's just like a girl, ain't it?
    To have you once then act like you were never there at all.

    My love is always wrong.
   Maybe there's a problem with the way I dress, undress things…
    My sad posture whispers "get lost" louder than "come-hither."
     But go figure.
I want to sleep f o r e v e r,   stay here till I'm g o n e .
        A heavy weight to hold! with these bedsheet arms…

Fingerprints are forever stamped across these shades,
        no matter how many times I've tried
    with this sleeve, with *his* sleeve, to dry clean
        the way the linger over, underneath.

Or maybe I want the sun
     to glass jar-house
          this Star's
               identity.

Maybe I want to wear his feral sores
        as secret battle scars
            acquired in some unknown ovicidal war,
   where impossible bonds were
      bent
          and breakable,
  and legal documents disguised
  no more   the utter nonsense
        they have always,   always been.

Maybe then, in this
    liquid field of scarlet absence
        it would make sense
          when I'm supposed to be running why
            I can't have him
       follow me, tread in my calling,
   or come
    back home to fall under
  this ten-foot-tall canopy, translucent green
        aqua sky…

    Drunk.

  When I'm not
       the only ladybird he's known
  with such freckled wings,
     paint-splattered in red sands
of abandon.

    Dreams.

Rafinesque Manatee (AKA The Stripper Anthem)

I swell

                with crimson light unbirth
                cradle the promised world

inside me

                dressed in salt-kissed mist
                of whimsy

(mystery)

                a seashell
                shroud of lore

Mythology

                opalescent crown of effervescent pearls
                and algae twin
                twist fisherman limbs around me
                catch me in black fishnet sultry wanton gazes
                lazy sun-struck iris of honey brown and me
                in twin black and white reflections—

My Image

                cast in hungry bubble eyes
                weighing the luminescent scales of my self-worth
                slippery
                sliding from high tide to low

elusive

White Light

        rainbow sunbeams from an afterglow

              Swim to me
             through me
               in me—

I will be

        your sparkling Sea Queen

You can call me

        Coral Flowers—

I will siren-sing you

        sweet blue melodies

You will feign belief

        in green coin harmony

   wish whiteout in black smiles like a

        Lighthouse

         Icon

            Legend…

                I will be
                  red-
                  bled.

                 I will
                 Reign.

Hey, Loser, Clean the Kitchen

I lost my words in a marble-floored oil spill,
    left my message on a countertop of wet regrets
  and post-midnight cravings.
I lost my turn of phrase to be yours,
        typed up.
I left my feelings in fabric,
    submerged in a watery grave.
I lost my words in a white sheet
    of misplaced carelessness—

                They were all about you anyway.
            I guess they never meant that much to me.

I Think We All Have Bad Tattoos

My name is changed
                                      to Someone.

    It's definitely better than
        No One.
    Or that (insert curse)
        over there.
So fine.
                                    I'll be
                                    Someone.

And if I find
I'm already taken
                                    I'll be
                                    Someone Else.

And I don't   bleed.
And I won't   bleed.
    That's what a guy said
    who used a needle in me—
    but it's not what you think—
    it was just a tattoo,
a mood,
    something permanent
    inked beneath the surface
                                    forever.
Shallow. Well,
my skin's known
    deeper   w o u n d s,
more cutting   l/i/n/e/s.

And hey, I look alright.
    So, I guess
I'm fine.
    This world thinks with its eyes.

The Moon Slit Her Wrists
by Sunset's Request for More
Color in the Sky

I don't believe in
magic anymore   the hope
I held it in me

waiting to be freed
all these glass pipe dream empty
promises of hushed

fairytales we keep
repeating under sheets of
soundwaves rocking warm

energy in our
inner spirit   hungry youth
desperate for a goal

to reach for   even
if the gold star's not there just
hanging by the moon.

I Need Therapy After Going to Therapy

They

    are the humorless ones,
        the eradicators   of alarm-sounding symptoms,
        not the erasers   of lethal dis-ease.

The execution of a ghost girl
        still ongoing,
            years past when the jury hung,
              defying gravity as just
                another
            breakable
              law.

      But let us braid your hair.

      But let us smear the colors of your mouth.

      That band of moods you feel?,
      There's a stone for that,
      vague instructions for give-and-take
      to follow.

      -Vindictively-
      annihilate the loser underneath!
      Kill!, Kill!

      Come back in a week.

      Smile.

      Tell us of your victory.

Four-Fifty is Greater Than Seven

What can I do to make it all better?
    To make it all fuck off to where is started from?

                                              Golly gee.
                        If I knew the answer to that riddle
                            I probably could've stopped
                              rhyme scheming my way
                                  out of my mind
                                    a long time ago.

Can't I call a friend on the phone?

                Well I was thinking about Sylvia Plath-ing it,
                    cranking the oven to four-fifty
        and shoving my face inside.
                  But for practical purposes,
                                yes.
                         I guess
            I'm technically every bit as capable
    of pressing seven digits on a plastic console
                  (inconsolably)
    and waiting for a might-as-well-be-stranger
           to slice the ring of future silence
              with a trite here-and-now
                              "Hullo?"

                      But I'm not here to lie to you.
                And whenever I'm here I lie to you.

Can't I write a list of ten things I'm infatuated with
     right
            now?

—Time
　—is
　—tick
　—tock
　—drip
　—drop
　—*g o n e.*

But that can be my first seven, right?

　　　　　　　　Please say yes.

Because the more stress I present
　　the more homework I'm given.

And this ain't real school.
And I've never known home in this
　　　　　　　　　　room.
And my hands stopped reaching for
　　　　　　　　vowels.
　　And now I've given you seven
　continents　　of asinine assignments
　　and you have yet to gift me
　　　　　　with a consonant,
only cheese grater to your smile,
　　hopin' I'd rebound that frown
with something a little more
　　　　　　happy.

　　　　　　So, how's this: Y e s.

　　　　　I can call a friend on the phone.

　　　I'm sure it will quell my quest
　　　　for destruction of self,
　　　　　of second best.

                              Just as well.
                    I'll give 'em hell.
I'll see ya in a week.

            Jesus Christ,
          something stinks.

             Oh, my Gawd,

      I forgot to turn the oven off.

                  See?

I told you I've lost my sentiments…
           or is it sensibilities?!

          Something's spilled.

            And it's burnin'

              underneath.

And Then I Got That Call About the Weather

It matters not how long it's been
thinking about you
always have a way back
inside my everything
takes on jazz mint rhythm with you
know how to change my mind
make it yours
is my favorite voice I've ever
used to the truth by now
I should know the feeling
lost inside this feeling
lost my mind
my habits break
slowly is the first undoing
what I shouldn't be doing
too much is never enough
of the real stuff
those feelings down
white comfort down
it all remains
forever unfound.

L o s t.

A g a i n .

W h e r e   i s   m y   S o u l ?

To Freeze

                              I lost
                    my virginity
              alone
                  with her
                        in my bedroom

      alone
a little flower
    blended
   bundled up
    beneath
     a tree
      left
     for me
all haste-y tied
and ribbon-less

 an Other's
  presence
too precious
 to breathe
  at once
a little hill
 should be
  enough
 too warm
  outside
 to freeze
  petals
too suddenly
  familiar
 to behave
 so alien

.   .   .

I descend
    the stairs
        like a plane

            c
             r
              a
               s
                h_____

metal wings
enfold
me asleep

dumb

like I drift
to school
the next day
on two feet

numb

when I told 'em
I have flown
before

like *hey*
it's cool

I felt

n o t h i n g

S'More Love

…And when we roast each other
it's like summer marshmallows,
    pillowed, soft.
    The sweetness sticks
because that's all we mean by it.
    Laughter lost in love—
                                      it's cool.

We never get charred
    by half-serious insults
about such stupid things—
    our quirks, pet peeves,
                                      because it's cool

to laugh at these oddities
    and minor annoyances
    others grieve
because we gave them grief!—
    Ourselves,
    uncensored, freed—
    because we trust
these kindred campfire spirits,
because we love these friends…

…We leave our hurt hanging
    in night smoke
    like a ghost story we've told,
like a jagged cliffhanger misspoke—
but we'll recite the staged fright once more
in time-torn, quilted, warm togetherness,
    because the way the plot melts
    and the timeline crumbles
        in our mouth…

                                      it's so cool.

I Used to Say Things Like "Casual Get Together." Wow.

Keep your house to yourself,
    just give me the party,
        just give me the home.

Keep your hands to yourself,
    just give me the holding
        onto enough longing to hold.

        Mold me
    into someone worth holding in yourself,
        your home.

            Fold me.
        Keep your clothes on,
    just give me the unfolding,
hampered laundry of soiled knees and ripped jeans.

            Spoil me.
        Tell me your story.
    Tell me what makes your mood ring
        blue, brooding.

    Move me.
    Transport us
on a stale breath worth holding for hoping
one day we'd actually be going
to some place worth knowing
in the folds of your head-and-heart home.

    Without ever owning a car.
    Without ever leaving this house.

Dug

Rooftop
    looks a lot
        like a cage
            above a room
                    full of crazy.
        A floorboard
            of dancer's leg to shindig in.
        Diving board
            to divide the end,
the then and now,
    post-perfect,
present tense,
        chillax
                trampoline.

We   circle 'round a movie screen,
clique the time   surfing stupid things.
Dumb sitcom plot,   rerun,   climax-free.

I   wanna see through film
    I always hear you lick 'n' love,
        some flick about a guy
            who Holy hates what he's afraid of.
    Fear
        the script will know too much of me.

                They say the concept's higher fire
                than the price of gasoline;
    ethanol can't haul the way up
    to brand this bottled can of understanding.
            You'd   need magic,
    too much room
        to crowd this

dumpster-fun-bar-standing-in-the-backseat,
take-and-break-the-backstreet
when-you-should-be-sitting-stone-free,
toll, tax the highway.
Pool your born-to-be-a-rebel metal body
to shop the forest, spore down doors with me,
belle James Dean.
Collect coronary alabaster sheets
in sea-foam-white umbrella guys—
and maybe then—

    we can wash our lightness
    in the faucet of these
    flat
    screen
    skies.

Unlock the orange juice carton clouds.
Level the playing field of ledge.
Comp the info-
clean commercials.
Jump in earth
to clear the hurdles.
Cracked stone wings watch freeze frame
on this cement bed.

I   can't read a word you said,
but think I understand the premise:
It would be so grave to end this.
Game play, no video,
fast rewind,   STOP!, forward go.
Yellow caution tape's a lame late witness,
the only shade I'll get by doin' this.
Post-live can't be recorded.
Kiss missed times and things distorted *all*... or not.
Ya dig?

We Flew to the Other Side of the World to Stand Outside the Planetarium

Sometimes I wonder if I might
      fade   into the Earth with you—
            I've been beneath the street before
                under different circumstances.
Strangers, vintage houses, candy skies, stars as planets.

  I was once alive,
      just as much as I could be,
                running   to make sense
  of all the   nothing
                  life drums in me.

    Sometimes the rush is crowd-less field,
    and sometimes the tar's observatory.

                            "Just you and me"
      feels so lonely,
    says the only familiar
      line that hits this empty
when I press "repeat" again.

        Even then, there's now,
           when I haven't learned
          my lessons like I thought I would.

  Somehow, I hear birds
  in the echo of you
                humming.
And I wonder if that's why
  I can't stop singing
      songs I think can paint the surface
         when I know I should be sleeping?

A Book Called Ghost Town

Red stands for Grand Canyon ghost town.
    Desert mountains, cactus highways.
        Full moon that hangs
            closer than a nightlight.
                Thirsty, deep piranhas
        desperate for a drink of Earth.
Spirit on the skyline.
    Powerful in powerless—
        only lightbulbs burn in stars.
Yellow bubbles on the stone, tar track
    before paths were paved that far back.
Vintage folklore,
    quaint font written in black books
held together by small hands.
        Twin beds for only children.
I see back to a time that knew the future.
I see lonely streets ahead.
              But you've walked these roads before,
                kicked rocks all the way back home.
Anything to steal your mind from the memory.
        Tumble's too heavy to be remembering
            how hard you hit gravity the first time
                you fell from Life.
Let's imbibe this one away
    to another blue so deep it divides the sky.

            Those were yesterday's bad habits.
        Those were an ever-stretching tomorrow's problems.
        This is a never quite arriving, never leaving today.
            Always ahead, read tales behind.
    Always not quite right.
    Not alright, but lying, always,

"Yes, I'm fine."

That was a good idea at the time.
That was a lie any idiot and I could see right through.

    This is cellophane.
This is bad wrap jobs,
        lousy hide-and-seek,
            recycled lyrics,
                and bad raps.
This is borrowing what's left
        without asking you
    to hold the blame as punishment
            for always staying
                with me
                  when I wanted you to
            leave.
    Wise One
        should be invincible,
            incapable of hurt.

This third rock eyes another planet
    with suspicion
    —or is it lust?—
Can't get enough insight to say.

Always outside my mind.

            But hey,
            I'll be fine.

                        I'll always be.

Some Thoughts from When I was Driving Home from Home the Other Day (It's a Long Story)

I've bathed in the piss of a million fish both dead and gone.
    I've decreed myself *Clean*
        when I knew I really wasn't,
            had no intention to ever be.
                "Just you and me—" how *lonely!*
                        I have a feeling I've hit that line before,
        totaled my Soul's worth
            as I was standing still.

What the hell is a brick wall?
    You mean the only thing left
    collapsing from the thought of me?
My breath could light your cigarette.
    And by "your" I mean "my."
        Which is to say
    my sustenance is selfish poison.

Sometimes I turn the light back on
            just to flip the switch and see
    how nothing the room becomes
        when I'm leaving.
Sometimes I remind myself
    it's childhood knocking on my memory's glass
        to throw the car door open, eject myself
    like a pirated videotape, become flimsy
                silk film ribboned on the highway.
How long I've held it in me!,
        this compulsion to un-be
            what keeps on being made.
It's as much love as hate.
But it's neither.

It's just apathy.

    Once, I learned the etymology of the word
    that calls the pain in your heart   "nostalgia."

                                  It's *nostalgia.*

Sometimes I want to paint my pain on other things,
    like all those yellow hills covered in green clouds.
You didn't know what I was talking about,
    so you told me to write it down
    by drawing you a picture.
I did.
    You couldn't decipher my drawing,
        and I decided I sucked at everything.
    I promised I'd never stop running
        until I could fly above the world
            on the weight of feathered wings.

                      When I got closer I learned
                          those clouds were trees.
              They look so cumulus from a distance,
                the accumulation of hurt from below.

Can you believe I live in them now?

Around Again

My Head — exclusive concert for your riffs and chords.

My Body — dirty playground for your lighter tricks.

My Face — field of poppies for your dreams to bloom.

My Heart — busy landfill of your former flings.

My Soul — tumbling laundromat
              of your bundled feelings—
                    Pockets stuffed with giving up,
                    buttons full of holding hope—
                    around and around they go…
                    eventually they'll come out

                          clean.

Four Fifty-Six AM with Thirteen Seconds Left

I stand butt naked in front of the mirror,
see the stranger of my smile,
try to brush the pain of carries away,
surf the waves of crowded space
for broken bottle messages,
debris…

Floss.

I put a hella good song on,
one that makes me feel stoned
even when I'm not.
One that was written for Someone Else.
(And I wish it were written for me.)
One that meant something to you
back then,

I guess.

And so, by default and dead memories
now it means something to me.

Or whatever.

It's been soundwave stalking me
for the better part of a week,
the very best of me…
And now I can't forget you
all over again.

*Guide my hips through riffs familiar,
let 'em rock 'n' roll right through me...*

I dance, just a little,
just to keep it movin'—
And I'm not sure I want the sands to wave us
"Bye"
in this direction,
wear clear crescendo downpour
in the sink
unsilently...

Spit.

But I'm not sure I want to stop dancing,
either.

I Say to the Girl…

I can't unveil summer
    from your eyes,
               untaste the salt of something sweet
                                        (so good!),
            unfly what freedom feels like,
                alive!,

  beyond my time pissing away
           on thirds
     and fourths
        and fifths
            into the morning.

                      I can't get hung up in posters
           on your wall
              of Popstars
                  and "fine" boys
                  and Conor freakin' Oberst,
     or the softness of teal felt rugs
          pooling me to shoot with you.
               Such a terrible aim,
     so unlucky as a magic eight ball.

  Meridian nights,
      the Hawaiian sound of your whistlin',
            cryin' along to guitar songs.

     Alone in act but not in theater,
                     with her.

I want a mirror,   this time one I won't break.

I want a wall   painted in your handwriting.

Not Much Like a Butterfly

Those dusty wings know
    porchlight, don't they?

                      Home
              through that door.

                              Offer of chair
                        to share your genes—

        you look a lot
        like a firstborn.

            Flesh, emotion.

Make believe that floor
    has held your ground before,
        your cigarette stale breath
                outside as we ashed the past
        of finer things.

            Every morning's a mistake
            with you.

        We got used
                to flicker feelings,

        inching,

    like every hardship sailing
                into livestream massive movie screens
        of color changed in rust,
                dressed in dust

                    cocoon.
         Bleeding sunrays of escape
        centered on the trauma's healing.
I wish I could believe
              your smile stealing headshots
                        from the curtain
                 cut to wilt with you.

                  Once,

    your hands made
              park bench
                    of my shoulder blades
                          as you said my name
                    in one
                 congruent ruse.

                  I wish
    every handshake
              knew how to loving touch me
              easy
                    on the outside,
         stealing blaze
    into my insides
              without ever leaving
                 a bruise.

                  And move.

The Cheapest Extermination

They say it's so
    inexpensive
to remove me
    from myself.
They've seen me
        get high
off heavy breathin',
            lifted to the ceilin'
lickin' shallow dishwater
    like a feline would.
            Concrete stoned
just by fallin' down with feelin's
        for no apparent reason
            and refusin' to get up again.

I don't need anything—
I don't need a helping hand
to handle leavin'
    myself on the doorstep
    of this bein' alive
        but for a season.

I've got this.
Under skin.

Very close
to sternum's surface
Burnin' coldness
    deep within.

It's like
    I'm g o n e
            before I begin.

When Sickness Steals These Nights

They tell me not to stand
                      before glass
                                    when I'm like this,
    under currents,
        an avalanche,
a storm
        of unforgivable
so memorable,
        but easily forgettable.

    I won't remember in a week
        how "strong" I was
           to use my hands and knees as anchors,
linoleum floor
    as beachy sand and shore.

I won't remember.
    But mind don't think that's what this space is for.

        Sometimes I want to, though,
    recall a sepia night
                with excruciating detail, accurately.
        That way, when I say
                "I could never forget,"
           I would mean it.
    And I wouldn't be lying again.
        On some stranger's couch,
                eighths of fifths
    into the morning
        quarry, no stone unfound allowed.

Not in ghost town.
                "Not in my house."

    I want to fill my denim pockets
                      with handfuls of tiny pebbles
       like the ones you used to kick
         back home from school
             beneath the mountain view's sky blue.
    I want it all to mean something to me
          like it did, you.

I want to not lose my way.
I want to feel this weight,
      know it comes from something that's not me.
I want to know I put it there all along.
I want to find something I can
    blame me on.

Firm Habits

Because we do this every day,

and we know now what works
to undo everything,
untie our likeness from the bullet list
outline of cut losses and silk ribbons
another color from the stripes that keep us
rigid, confined.

Because we do this every day.

And it's not fine, but now
we've started something rolled fast
past the finish line of sweet piano music,
ink-stained white sheets,
and whatever other means of almost nothings
we adhere meaning to.

Treble high-note Angels whisper-sing
us to sleep only then—when
limb-flying Maestro's left the pit of our Soul
filled with sharp-tempered edges
and flat-energied pulses.

Until then—we must hold
this swell beat

steady

in unsound

discord.

Rx Dreams

I met a man the same color as the wall.
He never blinked.
His corneas rehydrated themselves
with little feats of magic.

                                He's a thief.
He robbed my Mother
                   of her Nature,
the cornucopia of apple skins,
                the core belief of everything,
where the world begins,
                the essence of words and their lucidity,
faint belief
                that anything could be
just as it's meant to be
              said, without quantification.
                                    What,
                do I have measuring tape
                      unrolling yellow centas
                          from my tongue?
      Hundred meters yawn,
              bump the goose flesh
                    from my skin.
            Rose, let me in.
     Autopsy.   Thorn,
            take a flank of me.
There's piece enough
              for everybody
      willing and able
to dismember me,
              remember me incorrectly
when I'm sewn up hip-to-waist again,
                              in haste,
with all the space removed.

Let's Call it "Nightlife"

It might as well be mine.

The werewolves, warehouses.
These mothball rooms.
These high beam, ceiling-slung disco bombs.
These invisible drip-crystal chandeliers.

These shoe print hollow doorframes
    holding handshakes of a ghost.
        Chalk outlines pressed into the glass of time
by little cocaine clouds of breath-smoke.

It might as well be mine.

        These too thin blinds that ebb and flow
to purple rivers of nightlight in the night sky—

        let's call it
            "n i g h t l i f e."

These turquoise stones rockin' misnomers
    as seed as cherry pits,
        grasping at feelings like falling apples,
blinking the crawl of wake away,
    pretty thick like spider lashes.

These smack-gum-chewing,
    pink-wig-wearing,
glitter-eye-rolling,
    "X" hand,
        armband
    candy kids.

This menthol pack mentality

                of lost and lonely souls.

These hand-rolled sellouts.
      These unfiltered sellers.
            These distilled impurities
                  of might-have-been-better times.

All these garage band nineties
                  never minds.
These "too-suddenly-trendy-to-be-retro"
                  thrift store finds.
Black holly frames of sight I try on
      like to see with you
           is to hear the stars
                  unresting,
shoot with the firstborn bad boys
drumming up a rhythm that sinks
                      into me,
        forces my heart to beat
    in unison to its hit song—

            let's call it
                "i m p u l s i v i t y."

I told you, "I'll be fine," and thought the will to fly
      would rise me up.   Tonight.
I held your "get well soon," and I feel better now.   Alright.
To leave: unchosen option—one I still don't know how
      to lose completely.   Out of sight.
Oh, my mind!, I just really wanna move with you.
Sure, orbit 'round my hips, but I really wanna headbang, too.
   Man, I love this band!   Girl, can I have this dance?
      Yeah. Right.   And why not?
   My fever blends this rainbow white-hot.
   Freezes.   And bleeds.   My blood. My life.

           It might as well be mine.

Cokehead. Cigarette Butt.

Is that my butt
sitting on the ground?

Did I forget
to throw you away?

I'd Rather be Blind

Glowing, orange, octopus bar light
    swings on strings, stays shining,   bouncing on the powerlines,
throbbing with the impulse
                  to
                    break,
                                  dance,
              slide fever
                      through the screen.

The silent scream
            of staying awake all night.
The orb of twisting esoteric sheets
        tears into me,
                    a snare drum of dragonfly wings.
                      This underswell of liquid humming
fills me soft,
        even coming
    to a sun
            day morning,
    can't be unclothed
               in time.
    I try
        to bend my mind
                    inside
                          out.
                  I try
                      to shut it
                              d
                                 o
                                    w
                                      n.

              (It's so loud!)

Fast Fever Flying High

"And this, too, shall last
    long enough to wrap around me
        once, twice, thrice, maybe-*five*-times—"
Fuck!—
        and-that's-*excactly*-what-I-said-the-*last*-time-
            this-fever-found-me—
"FUCK!"

    Metal Mike once said
        it could all be justified if
            "The goin' up was worth the comin' down."
And-sometimes-I-think-it-*is*-
    and-sometimes-I-think-it's-not-
and-sometimes-it-*IS*-
    and-sometimes-it's-*SNOT!*

        Haha, "Snot!" like-that-clear-shit
            drippin'-from-my-nose,

        like-a-*drip-drip-drip-*
      clear-turn-to-red
    nosebleed-me-dead
Ohhh
Fuck.

    Sometimes the birds sing me to sleep at six AM
        because I-run-around-in-backward-circles,
    then ransack-the-fridge and freeze-the-ransom
            like an ice stick.
Because I popped
    three tires in
        two weeks all
            one block
                from *my* street

              because, well,
sometimes-I-just-don't-get-tired-till-the-sunrise.
Once, I unplugged *all* the machines to-save-electricity,
                              and because
I-HATE-THEIR-FUCKING-WARNING-BEEPS!—
                    But-then-I-realized-
              I'm-not-supposed-to-*do*-that-type-of-thing-
      because-I-*need*-them-
                    and-they-keep-my-heart-a'beat.
Oh. *Shit*. Oh, I'm sorry,
FUCK!

                Sometimes I want to scrape my knees on purpose
                    so the raspberries remind me
        that the soft wounds heal themselves
              and the deep ones   *never*   *find*   *me.*
Sometimes I listen to groups play under *band* names
        that should host a **trigger warning**
              and ditch their **trademark.**
Sometimes I want to tie a stranger's shoelaces
                                  into mine
            so I can say I tried
              to empathize,
      know all the things I *don't,*
        know all the things I *won't*—
recommend a book *I haven't read*
        the first *or* final pages to a friend-in-a-ship
            I didn't know had left the dock.

Oh-well-a'tick-tick-tick-tock, Cuckoo clock,
        you run in backward circles,
      you've got no time to talk—
        Fuck, "**You-silly-little-selfish-flower,-**
you-stupid-little-liar!
Go-back-to-kindergarten-
you're-gonna-stay-in-there-awhile-like-an-old—"

Fuck!
    I have a feeling I've done this before.
        I have a feeling this won't be the last—
"Time flies *fast* when you're high-on-life!"

                But *I*—
   am   *falling*
        now.

I have a feeling I've *done* this before.
I have a feeling this won't be the last

                          time.—

_____Beeeeeeeeeeeep!
                    Fuck.
_____Beeeeeeeeeeeep!
                    Fuck!
_____Beeeeeeeeeeeep!
                    FUCK!
_____Beeeeeeeeeeeep!
                    FUCK!
_____Beeeeeeeeeeeep!
                    I'M SORRY!
_____Beeeeeeeeeeeep!
                    I'M SORRY!
_____Beeeeeeeeeeeep!
                    I'm sorry!
_____Beeeeeeeeeeeep!
                    I'm sorry

My Moldy Smile

She swerved her auto body on the highway
    of human traffic,
        used   "I'm sorry" as a headlight,
        "Excuse me" as a brake.
Every sideways misstep,
    the epidermal touch of every would-be
    shoulder bump, erased
        by a few shallow words.
Well fuck that shit.
That was back then.
This is here, before us. Now.

        She stopped apologizing for slights
            of fiction.
    No more "Sorry" after every cough,
        "'Scuse me" after every sneeze.
            Beachy waves were cheap;
        she stopped brushing her hair.
        She forgot what her face saw
            with eyeliner on;
raised skin had supplied
an unworthy foundation to venture.
            She wore (or not)
    whatever she did (or did not) want
        to don by daylight to dusk
            in her own backyard.
        If you wished not to see,
        cork a hole in the fence.
    Don't get caught up in her rapture.
    She stopped shutting out slivers of sunlight
from beyond her bathroom window
        every time she took a piss.
    She didn't have care enough
        to obscure the splash of her life-force

                    hitting the water below with a hiss
                that could travel through waves of sound
                                    to your ear.
                    Here, here!
        Don't like her,   don't listen.
                            She was acid rock.
        Two drums, percussion, thousand l i n e s .
                            A too drunk live act
                            who shouldn't be live.
                    This was her house.
                    She swore with Gaw-damn gratuity,
                naked stretched with fuckin' fluidity.
        This was her pity party,
                did your tears poison the tea?
I drank it, but it wasn't meant for me.
I stopped apologizing for slaying
                your sleep,
staying unawake past noon.
I forgot to brush my teeth every day, twice a day,
        for three months in a row.
I no longer rinsed the perfume of Clear Spirit
        from my cavities.
    They got worse.   They hurt.

    This was your world smiling, I'd just cratered a hole in it.
                I stopped trying to fill it.
                    Again.
            I stopped craving to ungrave concavity.
                    Again.
        Bad things rained importance in zero gravity.

                    To hell with them.

Is She Shining?

I cry so hard
        I choke
on the swell of my senses,
      bloating my eyes
            as two
      useless,
      crescent
            fools,
too feelingly
to see
the beauty,
      pine for apathy.
Apparently,
pathetically,
      I fell
too hard,
too fast
to break
      my land
with open palm.
        My hand
cast
a fighting fist
thrown sideways
    after the fact,
        straight into me.

                I had to drive
              all the way home
                 with a bird
              stuck in my grill.

That bird
           was somebody's baby.
That bird
           was somebody's lover.
That bird
           was somebody's friend.

           The subject.
     The fluid painter of still life.
     The carpenter of highest shelf.
           The object
to cage the coveted out of reach.
           The cellar.
That bird was somebody.
           The watercolors.
Not the others, but the self.

           Exoskeleton.
           The shell.
           The underneath.

           I took her out.
     Midflight, white daylight.
           I took her down.
           I ended life.
Drifted all around with her,
The Shadow sides of a circle.

I hate
this town.
My fist hates
the side of my head,
Mahogany. Mondays.
I wish I didn't exist.
I always break
everything
I want.
I wish.

Crack Like a Geode

        I return her to the ground.
           Unsaid.
          Unflown about.
          Unusual shape.
        She stays in place.

Resounding mantra can't escape
the crown chakra call to rise up,
      be,
     reverberating,
     trembling
   like the dry clay earth
     retreating
into shallow graves again.

      Get out!, Now!, While you still can!

    At your own expense,
  by your own handmade omission
     of the artifacts.
      The sad attempt
       that went unnoticed,
        eroded fossil shells of past,
     but hey!,
  at least you tried.
This time, don't waste your wait
     on stupid things.
     Shallow things.
The display.
    Six orbits deep
    measuring your limbal rings
     with the exaction of DNA,
    memorizing the unique
     melanin array,

      the precise dose of primary colors
      that blend to claim the vision
in your eyes.
           Reciting lines…

                      (Burn the flesh!, Save the soul!)

            It sings,
            repeats,
        like any feather
             would
            in flight
          or terrified.

                        Clip the wings

                              like only

          T h e   O t h e r

                                  could.

Heave-ho the Clothes of the Hefty Ho

I stuff-and-shove-and-smash-and-shove-
and-slam-and-stuff-and-shove-and-smash
-so hard!-

My pants forget how to fit me.
My stupid gut's a swollen little selfish ship
taking on water,
robbing the very seas themselves
of their osmotic miseries.
(Not as miserable as me.)
Fifty-three pounds in a week.
The uncharted Science of it All
questions
the Phenom's believability.

Well.
It happened to me.

Zipper surrenders
to adhere my s p l i t n e s s
of mind
about the crotch—
more meager than metal,
feeling so much more
foil than steel.
So, I fuck off these stiff jeans.
Buttons cut
a new thread count
to s t r e t c h e d seams.
I unclasp the claw
that hooks me,
fat ho I am.
Make garbage of my garb.
Pasta sauce jar of my watering can.

My chest cleaves the upheaval
of lymph drainage clogged
down the mountains in the wrong direction.
My lung-filled back breaks
my flimsy bra strap just by breathin'.
No safety pin.

Nothing is sewn for me.
I stay strewn around naked for days.

Now ain't that heathen?
Now ain't that depraved?

The Zero's Prophecy

                      Sometimes I'm filled with so much wake
I want to Heroin myself to sleep.
            Alcohol in sick every day
                    for the rest of my life.
            Opiate every bottle
                  of this toothache pain away.
            Like these quicksand smile sifters
        missed the best of me.
Let me fall out
through mesh safety nets
        to rubber wet tar ground.
            Introduced me back to black box
                            dust again.
            The Alien.
        The Other
Me not Me
    from some back then.
My Only Friend
    who left me
             dry-heavin'
                  on the ashtray shores
              of heavy-breathin'.
Cup the staged wave
    of understudy
to second best.
        All these greedy hands
            upon your cigarette
                forgot how to cradle light.
Breathe those birthday wishes,
        exhale,
        let those names bleed sore free
            one more night,
                just *one* more flight.

Hold my hand.
    Take me higher.
        I won't tell anyone about us
                leavin'.
      I've got a fever feelin'
          it will be alright.
We will craft and carry
proud this plan
  to ripe fruition.
      It will be
        just y o u
           and m e
    this time.

      Let's call it

    "I n t u i t i o n ."

From My Mouth

I gave it back to you.
    Clear.
      Just how you gave it to me.
   Translucent.
        This time, a little bit more
  green-waved, salty
      splashing on my pillowcase.
I wasn't awake for it;
  I was sleepin'.
    It's the weekend.
  I call it Monday,
Tuesday,
     t h i r s t y
  e v e r y m o r n i n g.

    When you're not looking,
       I wash my glory in the garden.

           It's almost three PM.
           I let this night begin.

  I turn m y s e l f i n.   I turn the b l i n d s around.
I t w i s t i t o p e n.
P o u r i t d o w n. A b s o r b i t u p.
              P o u r i t d o w n.
   P o u r i t d o w n, d o w n, d o w n.
A b s o r b i t u p.   P o u r i t d o w n,
              d o n ' t p u t i t d o w n.
P i c k m e u p.   T u r n m e a r o u n d.
T w i s t m e i n s i d e o u t. L e t m e d r o w n.
   L i f t m e u p,   d o n ' t l e t m e d o w n.

B l a c k   m e   o u t.

Stillborn. Still Here.

This Dumb Bitch
  keeps breaking
    her bladder
    all over my bedroom floor.
She whines
    like whiskey-
    soaked country songs
        she hates
    and wails off key.
She's kinda high/strung/out
    for a guitar string,
        don't ya think?

I don't mean to harp,
    but she's a vapid thing,
        a "wish-I-could-forget-about-you"
            one night fling—
                burned acetone
                    in acid throat
                    every morning.
        A fleshy waist
of too much space.

        She falls down
            every three-past noon,
        dizzy,
    drives ceramic altar to her face.

        She needs to get out—
                    soon.

        She needs to leave
            me alone
                forevermore,

for the rest of my life on Earth.

The death she deserves
  is a slow burn, red from green.
    An endless one
      that spirals on,
        double-blind,
          continuously.

Hands and knees,
  hands and knees,
    she crawls.
      Infantile.
        Invalidly.

They said I shouldn't stand here now
  when I'm like this
    h e a v i n g .

        Don't look at me,
            you fucking bitch.
        Pack your bags.
            Get to leaving.

I SAID DON'T LOOK AT ME!

Icky Situation

I am not the sun today.
    Stardust,   but not the sun.

        I don't want the green behind the glass.

I blind that.

           Trees and ocean,
                so much ocean
      w a v e s
           me over   stones.

           I destroy a fashion show
                    in a magazine,
       cut paper threads
              of shattered rage on stage,
   doily efforts of everyone on the floor.
    Jagged little lipstick hearts
             and angular manifestos
scribbled   waxy red across   the corner of a mirror.

                  (You leave me, Chivalry,
             the one French door wide open.)

Find me

                       (lost and gone.)

   You are not my lover.
      Echoes of shell and sword
  knife feathered words circling the sky,
            spiraling under
                s t a c c a t o
                    i s l e s .

You lock your ivy needles 'round my trellis wrist,
pull me from my plan to "Stand!" and handle this.
   Remember...

I told you I put the "ick" in sick from the beginning.
And you tried to offer me sustenance.
I told you I put the "ick" in sick from the start.
And you tried to offer me "love," "peace of mind,"
a piece of your brain, not mine.
But I fast refused, said, "No!
I don't want to be so full of thoughts like you.
I want to be empty, clean, like me."
I told you I put the "ick" in sick before the warning signs
of bare bones flashed themselves like symbols and not side effects.
Before every trait was a chosen flaw in my person
and not the opaque Alien of this lethal dis-ease.
I told you, I've been hungry for a while.
You could hear the beasts in my stomach growl.
You tried to silence their screams.
You poured me a waterfall.
So, I took a sip of your mind, Spirit.
But it didn't fill me.   So, I took one more.
I told you, I've been sick for a while.
You pour, and you pour...

   I fall.

   I break   a column in a foreign land.
                                                (my bedroom)

You remind me there's a Place
       with machines waiting for me
       if I say
               "Yes."
                       No.   I won't go.

To Where Rain Hails

My feet swing high,
    suspended in midair
        like a child's would.

                No ground beneath them tumbling.
        I wade in hope
    support is there.

        I feel it—
        submarine,

forty-five degrees
    above falling,
        swallowing My Soul up into the calling
            of
                Some Not One of Us.

            Choking on the altitude of being
    a captive willing to pray for ceasefire,
        all victim demeanor released—

Retire.

So long they've bought me
behind the table of tribes
I was once
too young to know.

Fun
found my roots
in this strange
guy.

I'm coming home.

Metamorphosis: The New Girl

Become the girl

        who finds magic in an eight ball,
        fortune in a cookie,
        itinerary in a horoscope,
        colors not yet invented in a rainbow,
        a daughter in the sunshine,
        fairy wishes to hold time in dandelion seeds,
        luck in a ladybug,
        oneness in a four-leaf clover,
        new threads in a thrift store,
        Heaven cents in a gutter,
        quench in a broken bottle,
        trampoline in a mattress,
        maître d' in a hostess,
        playground in parched hills,
        filter faucet in a rainstorm,
        bathwater in a river,
"you-shoulda-been-there" stories in battle wounds,
beauty written in the scarred cells bundled underneath,
        stars in the sink,
        home in foreign lands,
        fairytales in what could never be,
        a give and take in chance,
        find the will to break
        to be free,
        flee…
        Find the girl
        to mind,
        unbury the splinters of peace.

Become the girl

        to find
        me.

In My Room

They let me keep the house to myself.
I can have it all.
Take everything.
They say it was just kept clean,
peroxide beat down any pathogens
in ammonia mortuary.

(Prescription protocol,
I can sense the essence.)

Black Jade petals
deck my bedside, ephemeral presence.
Delicate paper, ridge-filled cup.
No chipped crystal
in the chandelier above,
no flicker in the yellow-green
fluorescence.
No portraits framed
or hanging on the wall.
Blue rug rolls steps
that crawl
into a room
awash in mirrors.

"No thanks."

I don't need the extra stuff.
Cellophane-wrapped
temptation in the fridge.
Imitation "real life"
tour guide pamphlet.

      I'm sure I can handle it
                  on my own.
      I've been through
                  this town before.
      I've worn this city's blood
            like patchwork fabric,
                  hanging fashion projects
                              on a mannequin.

  I'm sure this will be
              enough.
  I can sound a bell
        for service
              if I change my mind,
        or if anything
comes up,
          or if anything
should happen
              to arise.

I'm sure
    I'll be
        alright.

I'm sure
    I'll be
        just fine.

Other Things That Make the Fall
a Tumble Worth Tripping

I bind a book about us all.
    It spells in symbols I've never seen before,
    makes words of characters I've never used.
My fingertips roam a wall that's pandered,
    primeval as humankind itself—and cast its touch in plaster.
I descend a handmade hill that's been beaten down
                            many times before.
                    It still stands with crucifixions.
    Stares on stairs,   *tears every time they tear it.*
I home-cook breakfast in a hotel bedroom.
        I microwave.   I leave cold oatmeal on the plate.
            A blond boy hands me a black umbrella.
                    His name is the same as everyone else's.
We storm storefronts before the rain has started.   I laugh.
I (((p-O-p))). Glass bubbles lift halos around me. Remembering
    Molotov cocktails came Russian like his last name
        through the bedroom window. They (still) don't know.
                It's (too) late (now.)
Handlebars blend me, abate me, tender as limelight.
        Sugar, agave, then given away.
    Let's say   my lungs are cosmopolitan,
                  eighty-three percent water and ash.
           There's still room for more in me. Sink.
           I find a plastic mask so bodiless.
    No-eyed pinwheel spokes.   *Look!,* it's my effigy.
Stoked, you rail tracks through the crosswalk,   like you
    were trained to be. Think: Soul-hungry. Unending. Need.
Striped awnings crystal-drip the image of my insides.
        Lightning   hits the same vein twice.
    A chord is struck. A promise. Sentence.
        Is this progress?, Is this music?
        Half Day Demolished.   New Age Blues.
                          "I see you."
    Down moods can't believe it's you.   You prove.
        You do look a lot like yourself,   don't you?

Just What I Wanted

Every time
        I hear this song
I see your face,
        you beautiful flower,
                you desert craft full of crazy,
                      you delicate strength
        still standing
                through disaster,
                      you pink walls
                      of Rothchild,
        you sunshine,
                Chateau.

I watch you wink
        with "I-could-give-a-care-less"
                              essence.
        I let you flirt
                with the Ones
        good fortune
                made for me.

(Love denied,
unfortunately.
See, Life lacks the coherence
to cut into me,
—or-is-it-I-it?!—
yells, "STOP!," betrays,
raids my speech. Stays quiet.
Oh well. I'm just as well in silence.
I'm a knife blade, cat scratch, accident.
Paper wings.
It's too heavy to wear the weight of me like sequins,
Halloween costumes, iridescence, UV glow stick things...)

Fast rewind the time—I would,
if given the opportunity.
I'd become Someone
a l i (v) e   to waste lipstick on,
resolve slate's skyline rose in me.
Hear the hush move through your hair,
dust, airbrush mine on other things.
Swim. Heir, this kiteless butterfly
of ancient absence,   absolved strings.
She once gave me a   l/i/(n)/e
                      that hit me
                harder than I thought
                    it could.

" If I can't be the One—
        —to love the memory,
promise me—
        —you'll become Someone—
            —to write the elegy—
—of every concept overplayed,—
        —misunderstood—
            —and out of mind. "

I have to sit,
shake hands with this.

I used to know you.
You're not dead.
(*They say I've moved on.*)

You will Never invisibly avoid me
in the Isles of Misery Again.
Nor I you.

And like any good song:
What if who I wanted
was a concept
all along?

Tear the Wait

                                I wander the corridors
                                past bunkers not mine
                                or meant for me.

The arcade's a coin-guzzling machine,
        one cohesive, uproarious greed.
                Plastic guns swing with ill-intentions—
upholstered little loveseat
    could hurt somebody!
Birds ask me questions
    in the foreign language of Avian,
angle pulse of neck
  to pose impossible equation—
                            me plus/minus me.

                Equality.
                Abstraction.
                Zero Angel
        in black combat boots.
                  Skid.
                Traction.

                I fast,
        make Michelangelo
    of rushed art in the streets,
find faded price tags of freedom
      in pastel scribbles
smothering government buildings.

                        Sand the white beaches
                            of ancient cities
                whose gutters proudly decree
                              their calling.

                              Pour L'Amour from tea kettle
                                       bubbles in brick.
                                  Art-strong urban walls
                                  silence my Soul's critic
                                      with denture, spine,
                                  and broken backspace.

          Virgin Mermaid carved her craft in stone.

I frequent cafes alone,
     tell the host,
          "I'm waiting for Someone…"
                                                (back home)

Order black coffee and cake
     outside
          on the patio.
     Excuse myself
          inside
               to the bathroom.

          Stand in the sink.

          Open the window.

          Slide through the screen.

                                             Leave.

My Likeness Looks a Lot Like You

The globe's a little goblin
    dismissed of his robe.

                                       I'm a fleece,
                         in and of herself.
               An undertaker of many rolls
                       of loose belt buckle,
        flesh
                that sinks
                          elastic
              from the hold
                   of skeleton
                   too stretched—
        pathetic framework
        for a theater of stars.

            These stars—
        each one of them ain't me.
          Someone Else once
          told me they believed
             we'd fall
            into them again,
          ascend our steps
         as medicinal taps
             on vertebrae,
         upward spiraling.
But what the French
    do they know, anyway?
    They don't
        speak for me.
There are seven billion
    counting ways
        to be lonely
    in this world with you.

  To miss Someone.
        Call them "gone"
    when they're still
        in the same room.
To inhabit
    the finished product
        out of habit.
So much practice
        putting on the painting.
The pain it takes!
        to wear an image
           that's not yours,
           was never drawn
                to be.
    I don't think
        it's a "luck of the draw"
           to be lucky;
I think
    that's up to me,
        how I choose to see myself
                    flying
                as I struggle
            to find overhead
        warm enough
           to hug me,
      yet open enough
        to let me
                soar, continually.
    I've seen cerulean
  rule blue the outcast,
        dismiss the hue
  for a better mood,
    a brighter truth
ringing
    beyond the bell sleeves
        of evergreen trees.

I've been tangerine, too,
    in moments
        that reminded me
            forever less of "I"
and so much more of you—
                      happy.
Peachy with the comfort of knowing
        —whatever happens between us splitting—
            there's always a thread
                          hanging,
                      waiting
                to sew you up,
match the color of your mood
        in the morning.

Return of the Roach

In the beginning, there were the roaches.
    They say those buggers could survive atomic bombs,
               nuclear warfare.
        And after a spinning past
            of NorCali-born-NOLA-childhood-livin',
I believe 'em.
    Mama home alone
        afraid to coast into the kitchen
                because
"I don't know where that damn thing went."
    Queen sleepin' upside down in a King's bed,
        only weapon
        the stepped-on sole of a left shoe
            in her right hand.
Yeah, I believe 'em now.

Her spirit animal must've been the roach itself.
Weird totem, but whatever.

I let her out
    to fly about my Living Room,
    steal the blue from my gray windows,
    pain the runoff that my soul shed
    then complain about the weather.
        Interlace her curtain hand in mine,
        whisk me from my pink bedroom
        of walled innocence
        into something…
    innocuous,
        frozen,
            rumbling in the cupboards,
                light footsteps on the floorboards
                      of wondering,
"Is-this-the-kinda-stuff-they-make-pixie-dust-from?"

Wondering
        if silver spoons,
                white frosting,
            and ice chips would be enough.
                              Wondering…

They locked that bug-eyed bitch
in a jail cell for a crime she didn't commit.
        Swingin' sugar low like a chariot
                in the throes of the Valley,
                      high tech as a habit,
                            fool as a moonrise,
                                    noon.

They let her out again.
She stayed quiet then.
She shut up long enough
for them to forget
the sound of her voice.

But I
      still heard her whisper.
            I still sang with her in the shower.
                She still saw me naked,
                      ran her legs around me like Arachnid's,
                like silver spiderwebs
            on cold heartbeat machines
        by breath-slung fields,
            ribbiting alone past midnight,
                        croaking for rest…

I guess you could say I knew her best,
maybe better than I knew myself.
    Although she whispered,
                    she was LOUD!

She demanded her own shelf of affection,
    a storage place in my ribcage
        for the gold of her won trophies,
            the weight of her goals.

            I designated myself the loser
        who would drive her home,
    cake-lessly celebrate her small victories
            —slowly spending me—
        while just once
wishing I could unbuckle the ghost in the passenger's seat, crash!,
      let the airbags claim what they own.

                        She overpowered me.
            She'd kiss me sweet as honey-sunrise
              then leave me all day pillow-wasted
                    on my own bad habits.
                          She was spitfire.
                  She was fun-less tunnel vision.
                            She was rage
                       in beige tapestry
            of topless, taupe-caramel skin,
                salty over past remarks
                swimming in the same veins
                      those bugs buried in.
            Her arms were cinnamon-stick-red
            full of cross-stich from a knife tip's
                            blazing rain.
        She was vile,
                vital.
        She was a twig.
                She was vain.

She ran daily marathons of binge sleeping
in the basement, 'wake
from midnight till four, five, six AM.
She muted the black screen,
used its blue light to illuminate
the shadows cast by raised stucco sections
on the wall—
her checkerboard dancefloor,
her spiraling dining hall.

She smoked cigarette butts
bummed off the city's sidewalk,
drank the (probable) piss
scraping the bottom of empty beer bottles—
and she *hated* beer!
Once,
    I saw her feed from the trash can of a crowded theater aisle.
    Maybe life tasted deeper by twelve orbits lashing near.

She could still dry spit the Clear Spirit of last week,
stench scratching at the back of her throat.
Cheap cologne only exacerbated her allergic reaction.
Porcelain was religion.
Toothbrush, a magic wand.
    If I had three wishes
I would rinse her
        —green
        —all
        —gone.

She chalked the outline of my manuscript,
read the blueprint of her split demise.
Desert eyes unscrambling
the scattered bird shells of her homicide
scathed me
as I escaped for life—or tried.

        I have tried to kill her many times before.

                For years!,
                For years!,
                For YEARS!,

Her yoke drips unrelenting orange fury.
      Her legs hiss in hindsight,
          running, cycling circles,
              lamenting she's celestial dust—

                            and always will be.
She will never go home.
    She will never leave me alone.

                  Still!,
                  Still!,
                STILL!,

                                To this day,
              healing crystals are a gospel,
            wooden beads, a reminder I tried.

          To untie   this night,
         I undressed   my skeleton—
       exotic, if not an unusual site.
       I   fell   alone with her
      in a hiccup of consciousness
          beneath the rafters
           of a ceiling fan
               sky.

Not before I disrobed the hard layers I left her in—

      the nauseous bathwater,
           two!-sixty-*two!* pointed steps of inertia,
                the inane nerve ending's foreshadowing,
                the cold sweat glitter,
                    the shiver,
                            the sheer fear
                      her apparition would appear
    sudden!,

a smokescreen from the braille in the wall—
    two black eyes
        forever warring back a truce of lies,
absent pigment
        in her tardy flesh,
soldered handshake
        welded around my neck…

                And she *HISSES!*…
                And *HISSES!*…

                    Still.

www.ingramcontent.com/pod-product-compliance
Lightning Source LLC
Chambersburg PA
CBHW051649040426
42446CB00009B/1057

www.ingramcontent.com/pod-product-compliance
Lightning Source LLC
Chambersburg PA
CBHW051652040426
42446CB00009B/1107